Gleanings of Archer Road

Joseph Hamzik

Gleanings of Archer Road

Joseph Hamzik

First Printing: 2013

ISBN 978-1-304-45028-9

Contents

Acknowledgements

The Clear-Ridge Historical Society would like to thank the Hamzik Family for the permission to publish Joseph's manuscript. We would also like to thank the Chicago Public Library and The Chicago Historical Society for allowing us to obtain copies of the original manuscript from their collections.

A special thanks to Clear-Ridge Historical Society members Jennifer Lody and Janet Bitunjac for their contributions in painstakingly typing the original text.

Foreword

The history of Archer Road, told here for the first time, is a long and interesting story spanning from the time of the first Native Americans to the time this manuscript was written. It served as a portage route for native Americans and explorers, an access road to monitor the building of the Illinois and Michigan Canal, a stagecoach route, and a host of other transportation purposes. Mr. Hamzik's history will describe each of these uses in detail and enlighten the reader to the importance of this great transportation highway.

Joseph Hamzik was born on June 2, 1918 in Chicago and grew up in the Brighton Park community of Chicago. He was a 1933 graduate of Kelly High School and served in the US Army/Air Force from 1943 to 1945 where he was a gunner and airplane mechanic. He was a longtime member of the Archer Road Kiwanis Club and American Legion Post #271. Mr. Hamzik worked for the Chicago Park District for over 30 years. During his life Mr. Hamzik wrote over 300 historical articles about Brighton Park and the surrounding areas which were all published in the Brighton Park/McKinley Park Life Newspaper. Joseph Hamzik passed away on November, 6 1949.

This manuscript, Gleanings of Archer Road, was written in December of 1961. It is the culmination of years of research Mr. Hamzik did regarding the Brighton Park community. The manuscript was donated to the Brighton Park Library and eventually to the Special Collections Department of the Chicago Public Library as well as the Chicago Historical Society where it sat for many years.

The Clear-Ridge Historical Society decided to publish the manuscript beginning in 2012 after obtaining permission from the Hamzik family who always wished to see Joseph's work in print. The Clear-Ridge Historical Society has not changed any of the original text, only corrected a few minor spelling and grammatical errors.

The Clear-Ridge Historical Society Board of Directors

Robert Bitunjac
Ed Kozak
Dianne Johnson
Bruce Beveridge
Robert Russo
Paul Walenga
Bob Kott

Chapter 1: Historical Obscurity

Volumes have been written about legendary Indian trials, leading in all directions from Chicago, that were inherited by the early settlers, and contributed to the development of the city. Their history has been minutely recorded, with the exception of the thirty mile long, Archer Indian trial, running from 1500 South State Street in Chicago to Lockport, Illinois. The many colorful activities along this thriving route were obscured to historians by the publicity given newly tapped regions outside Chicago, reached with the introduction of the revolutionary plank roads and railroads. The chain of events that buried the history of Archer Road, had its beginning while early Chicago was standing still from 1816 to 1825. Great numbers of emigrants were pouring over the Allegheny fountain, and down the Ohio River into Kentucky, Ohio, Indiana, southern and central Illinois. Many of them helped popularize the Vincennes Trail, from the rich Wabash Valley to Chicago, which in 1849, encouraged the construction of the Southern Plank Road, ten miles in a northerly direction.

Gradually, settlers made their way into northern Illinois, feeling somewhat secure by the Indian treaties signed with their Federal government. The earliest settlements along to the Illinois and Mississippi waterways, the route discovered by Marquette and Joliet back in 1673. This became the most ancient thoroughfare out of Chicago, recognized as one of the five great keys of the continent, something the St. Lawrence system with the Mississippi. Unfortunately, the memorable events along the Archer Indian trail, adjoining this route, had been scantily summarized by historians, as a legendary Indian trail and nostalgic stage coach route. The plaudits fall flat for failing to recognize the great contribution Archer Road made in the early development of Chicago. By 1836, of all the early overland routes leading to the city, Archer Road was the first graded road for a distance of thirty miles to Lockport, long before the introduction of plank roads and railroads. The major improvement to the road took place in conjunction with the digging of the adjoining Illinois and Michigan canal, and thereafter, the route became a most popular commercial thoroughfare.

To the west and northwest of Chicago, the Rock River and Fox River Valley regions, remained sparsely settled because of the Indians. The few towns that did exist, had no outlets to Chicago, and were placed at a commercial disadvantage. When the Indian problem was finally resolved, demands were raised for roads, so as to compete in the trade established between Chicago and settlements to the south and southwest, reached by the Vincennes and Archer trails. As a result of their growing needs and unceasing clamor, the necessary legislation was secured, and corporations were formed for contracting plank roads and railroads, to tap the regions, west and northwest of Chicago. In 1850, the first Chicago railroad reached Elgin, known as the Galena and Chicago Union Railroad. The Southwestern Plank Road was constructed in 1848, leading to Barry's Point in Riverside, Naperville, and Oswego, becoming today's Ogden Avenue. Another new route that became today's Lake Street, was the Western Plank Road, completed in 1849, that led to Elgin and Rockford. The last of the improved routes into the newly tapped region was the Northwestern Plank Road, also completed in 1849, that led in the direction of the Fox Lake region, that followed a similar course of today's Milwaukee Avenue.

During this revolutionary building period, the history of Archer Road became obscured, buried by the publicity of the new routes. It continued to be a thriving thoroughfare leading to the city, long after the plank roads and the adjoining Illinois and Michigan canal were abandoned. Archer Road's commercial history spans one hundred and thirty-five years, dating back to 1827, when Archibald Clybourne purchased cattle at Hickory Creek, as intended provisions for the Fort Dearborn garrison, and were led down this route to the early settlement on the shores of Lake Michigan. In all these passing years that precedent has not been changed, as contemporary cattle trucks still traverse over nostalgic Archer Road, to the adjoining Chicago Union Stock Yards. "Gleanings of Archer Road" is the resurrection of its colorful history of yesteryear, reviewing many interesting facets, such as its commercial importance to the development of early Chicago, as well as the many integrated arterial roads branching from it, and the contribution of the regions from whence they came that popularized the use of Archer Road. Uncovering the sands of time revives the adventurous episodes of the Indians and settlers along its route, as well as heralding the exploits of many colorful personalities, such as Colonel William Beatty Archer, for whom the road had been named. Also reviewed is the transportation over Archer Road, once possessed with all the charm of a frontier saga during the nostalgic stage coach days, followed by the horse-drawn cars, the electric trolley, and the contemporary bus.

Chapter 2: The Earliest Indians

The authenticity that present Archer Road was once an Indian trail was established by historian Albert F Scharf In 1900, who indicated the route on his officially accepted map, titled, "Indian Trails and Villages of Chicago in 1804." The Chicago Historical Society, as well as Milo M, Quaife, author of "Chicago Highways, New and Old", also acknowledges that for countless generations, numerous Indian tribes drifted up and down the winding Archer trail, moving between Lake Michigan and the Illinois River.

It is difficult to imagine that back during the last glacier age, 10,000 to 25,000 years ago, sluggish rivers of the Arctic ice created a temporary land crossing between Siberia and Alaska at the Bering Strait. Anthropologists have long agreed that this intercontinental bridge vanished when the glacier was crossed by the earliest known North American settlers, who moved far down the continent in search of game. These people, largely of Mongolian stock, developed into those we now know as Indians. As they returned north, following the receding glaciers, their initial culture was called the Paleo Indian period, with its fluted points of shipped stone for spearing large animals. This period ended about 7000 B.C. The Archaic Boreal Indian era followed, with its woodworking tools of ground stone that lasted to about 500 B.C. From then on to about 100 B.C. the general vicinity of the Archer trail was occupied by groups of Early Woodland Indians, who although they still lived by hunting and fishing, they were the first people in the region to use pottery of fired clay, and to erect burial mounds over their dead. In the Middle Woodland period, lasting to abut A.D. 800, there was a cultural climate brought about by the arrival of the Hopewellian Indians from the Illinois River Valley. They were associated with the widespread trade and commerce with distant lands, and they showed artistic achievements that were never surpassed by later Indians. This was the period that agriculture had its beginning in the prairies surrounding the Archer Indian trail.

In the Late Woodland period, from A.D. 800 to 1600, there was an increasing difference of cultural groups in the region embraced by the Great Lakes. During a particular warm spell, around the year 1000, some new groups entered the local area from farther south, via the Mississippi Valley and its tributaries, as other groups came from the East, and all made their living by hunting and fishing. The Miami Indians, who had migrated from their original homeland in the Illinois Valley, came to occupy the region by 1671. Their language, manners and customs were almost identical with those of the Illinois Indians, and are supposed to be the parent race, or an important branch of that nation.

The Frenchman, Perot, visited this section in 1671, and found "Chicagou" to be the residence of a powerful chief of the Miami's. "The number of trails centering all at this spot, and their apparent antiquity, indicates that this was probably for a long while the site of a large Indian village." Father Marquette found them here when he returned to Chicago in 1674, and gave evidence that the Archer Indian trail was in existence at that time. Camped close to the junction of South Damen Avenue and the South Branch of the Chicago River, just three-quarters of a mile north of present Archer Avenue, he wrote; "Several Indians passed yesterday on their way to carry furs to Nawaskingwe." This would certainly indicate the existence of a trial. The closest to Marquette's encampment, as indicated on historian Scharf's Indian map, was the Archer Indian trail.

By 1685, the first white man made permanent residence on the shore of Lake Michigan, for there is a record of a fort having been established by Durantaye, a French official. The site on which this fort was located was later the place chosen for the erection of Fort Dearborn in 1805. The Miami Indians were still the dominant tribe of this region in 1708, when a French visitor at a local village wrote; "It was a real pleasure to see the Miamis occasionally bringing into their village some enormous bear, tame in the course of their hunting, and driven before them with switches, like sheep to the slaughterhouse." The Archer trail was a common scene with Miami's traveling on foot, with their woman carrying their burdens on their backs by means of headbands and pack straps. There was some use of dugout canoes on the Desplaines and Chicago Rivers, adjoining the Archer trail, but by and large, the local Miami's were not canoe people, like the Potawatomies from Green Bay, who were to descend from their northern habitat, and replace the Miamis in this region.

Chapter 3: The Iroquois Intrigue

The abundance of game surrounding the Miami villages and camps, on and adjoining the Archer trail, attracted an enemy from the East, who stealthily made his encroachment westward into the local hunting grounds. An early foe of almost all the Indians in the Midwest was the Iroquois Confederation, who constantly send war parties into this territory. Their early relations with the English along the Atlantic coast made them allies of the British during the Revolutionary War. The Iroquois invasion westward was to maintain their commercial advantages. They had long traded with the Dutch and English of the New York, who gave them in exchange for their furs; the guns, ammunition, knives, hatchets, kettles, beads, and brandy. When their game became scarce, they had to seek their beaver and other skins in the territories of the tribes they had to destroy.

Starting in about 1642, they eventually destroyed the Hurons; exterminated the Neutrals, and the Eries; reduced the formidable Andaste, to helpless insignificance; swept the hoarders of the St. Lawrence with fire, and spread terror and desolation among the Algonquins of Canada. They then turned their direction to the Illinois country, inhabited in the north by the Miamis, and the Illinois country, inhabited in the north by the Miamis, and the Illinois Indians to the south, both allied in language, manners and customs. It was always the policy of the Iroquois to first divide and then conqueror. They succeeded in the creating tensions between the two local tribes, which was revealed in Father Marquette's diary, dated January 26, 1675. He made the following entry during his winter encampment at South Damen Avenue and the Chicago

River, adjoining the Archer trail; "Illinois brought us on behalf of the elders, 2 sacks of corn, dried meat, pumpkins, and 12 beaver skins; 1st to make a mat; 2nd to ask for powder. I replied, and I did not wish them to begin war with the Miami's."

The plan of the Iroquois had the encouragement of some white men, who were enemies of the Frenchman Robert Cavalier LaSalle, and hoped to ruin his established fur trade in this region. The wealth of evidence revealing the existence of French fur trading along the Archer trail, would indicate that LaSalle having established the first trading posts in the region, was familiar with the nostalgic route. His historical trek through the Mud Lake portage, adjoining the Archer trail, was recorded as taking place about December 23, 1681. Historian Parkman described his local movements very briefly; "It was the dead of winter, and the streams were frozen. They made sleds, placed on them the canoes, the baggage, crossed from the Chicago to the northern branch of the Illinois, and filed in a long procession down its frozen course."

Finally, the Iroquois fell upon the Miami's and Illinois Indians in open warfare that continued for many years. The conflict harassed the French in maintaining their established trading posts. As late as 108, DeCourtemanche, an agent of the French, had visited the Miami's at Chicago, to induce them to cease their war with the Iroquois, which prevented communications between French Louisiana and Canada. Gradually, the tide changed against the Iroquois, by the growing strength of the Miami's, who had formed a confederacy with the Kickapoos and the Illinois tribe. Finally the enemy was forced to retreat, and were never again a threat along the Archer trail.

Chapter 4: Come the Potawatomie

With Iroquois cession in sight, the principal Miami chief, Chichikatalo, agreed to accompany the Frenchman to Canada, to make peace with them. As he reached the vicinity of Green Bay, he was attacked by the Foxes of that region. Then other enemies quickly appeared against the local Miami's. By 1714, even the Kickapoos became allied with the newly formed confederation of Foxes, Potawatomies and Sauk.   Major Forsyth, who lived a large portion of his life among the Indians of Illinois and Iowa, said; "These Miami Indians were attacked by a general confederacy of other nations, such as the Sauk's and Foxes, who resided at Green Bay, and on the Wisconsin; the Sioux, whose frontier extended south to the vicinity of the river Desplaines; the Chippewa's and Potawatomies from the lakes; and also the Cherokees and Cheetahs from the South. The war continued for many years, until the great nation was destroyed."   The Miami's who succeeded in escaping the onslaught, found new homes on the St. Joseph, the Maumee, and the Wabash Rivers. With their departure from along the Archer trail, a number of northern tribes came to roam the Chicagoland prairies.

By the early part of the eighteenth century, the Potawatomie's from the Green Bay region, had migrated south and became the dominant tribe in this area. Like the Ottawa's and the Chippewa's, the Potawatomie's were of the same Algonquin linguistic stock, and at sometime were likely one nation. In 1769, the Potawatomies joined with other Indian nations in their warfare against the Illinois tribe to the south, in order to avenge the death of Chief Pontiac, who had been treacherously slain by one of them. Referring to Scharf's Indian map, revealed that a number of Potawatomie villages, camps, and forts, on and along the Archer trail. Villages were located near Summit, at the Sag Outlet and at Joliet, with smaller camps at Willow Springs and Lockport. Another large village adjoined the trail at Palos. Three Indian forts were known to be located on Signal Hill, an abrupt rise of ground at Maple Lake, near 96th Street in the present Argonne Forest Preserves, another at the Sag canal and LaGrange Road, and the last in Palos at 103rd Street near 86th Avenue. When the local Potawatomies advanced against the Illinois tribe and surrounded them at Starved Rock, they more than likely traveled over the most direct route, the Archer trail to Lockport, continuing from there to the historical site by the Ottawa trail.

Some years after the defeat of the Illinois Indians, the local Potawatomies joined the confederation led by the Miami chief, Little Turtle, fighting the Americans as far [?] as Ohio. They were decisively defeated by General "Mad Anthony" Wayne, at the Battle of Fallen Timbers in 1794, which broke the power of the northwestern tribesmen. Of the chiefs and warriors from this region who signed the Treaty of Greenville with Little Turtle, were Winnamac or Wenamene, who became a close friend of the white traders and settlers about Chicago afterwards. Suggamu, or Black Bird, who later was the chief actor of the Chicago Massacre in 1812, was also there.

With its victory over the Indians, the infant United States government made its entrance into the old Northwest Territory. Realizing the strategic importance of the Chicago-Illinois waterway, adjoining the Archer trail, their price of victory over the Potawatomies in the ensuring Treaty of Greenville in 1790, was the free use of the waterway, from the mouth of the Illinois to Lake Michigan. The Indians ceded to the government a "piece of land six miles square at the south of the Chicago River." A beginning to safeguard the region was made to this end with the construction of forts along its route. Fort Dearborn was erected at the mouth of the Chicago River in 1805. The purchase of Louisiana from France in the same year, gave the waterway added importance to the United States. Down it, in the spring of 1805, came Colonel Kingsbury with a company of troops from distant Mackinac, to establish Fort Bellefontaine, opposite the mouth of the Illinois. The two adjoining forts came a link in a chain of outposts, set to guard the frontier, from the Mackinac to the Gulf of Mexico. As increasing pioneers and soldiers ventured over the Archer Indian trail, between these two outposts, it was gradually transformed into a road of the white man.

Chapter 5: South Fork of the Chicago

During the War of 1812, the local Potawatomies sided with England, and perpetrated the memorable Fort Dearborn Massacre, April 7, 1812. Many of the participants in that onslaught more than likely came from the nearby villages and camps located on the Archer trail. In her book, "Wau-Bun" (Early Days), Mrs. John Kinzie said that about five hundred half naked savages armed with muskets, knives, and tomahawks, fell upon the white settlers, soldiers, and Indian guides. Mrs. Kinzie wrote; "Runners had been sent to the villages to apprise them of the intended evacuation of the post, as well of the plan of the Indians assembled to attack the troops."

In the same year that the Fort Dearborn was rebuilt, in 1816, the Potawatomies were forced to cede the land between the two outposts, a long strip from Lake Michigan to the Fox and Illinois Rivers, twenty miles in width. Shortly thereafter, the popular use of the Archer trail came to light in 1821, when the government proposed to extinguish the Indian title to that portion of the country lying between the north boundary of Indiana and the Grand River in Michigan. A council to effect this object was appointed to be held at Chicago in August 1821. Governor Lewis Cass of the Michigan Territory, and Solomon Sibley were appointed United States Commissioners, and Henry R. Schoolcraft was named as their secretary.

Mr. Schoolcraft, in his work titled, "Travels in the Central Portions of the Mississippi Valley", published in 1885, gives a full account of their arrival is Chicago over the Archer trail. He wrote; "On crossing the Desplaines (Summit), we found the opposite shore thronged with Indians, whose loud and obtrusive salutations caused us to make a few minutes halt.

From this point we were scarcely out of sight of struggling parties, all proceeding to the same place. Most commonly, they were mounted on horses, and appareled in their best manner and decorated with metals, silver beads and feathers. The gaudy and showy dresses of these troops of Indians, with the jingling caused by the striking of their ornaments, and their spirited manner of riding, created a scene as novel as it was interesting. Proceeding from all parts of a very extensive circle of country, like rays converging to a focus, the nearer we approached the sore compact and concentrated the body became, and we found our cavalcade rapidly augmented, and, consequently, the dust, confusion and noise increased at every by-path which intersected our way. After crossing the South Fork (at Archer and Ashland Avenues) of the Chicago and emerging from the forest that skirts it, nearly the whole number of those who had preceded us appeared on the extensive and level plain that stretched along the shores of the lake, while the refreshing and noble appearance of the lake itself, with vast and sullen swell appeared beyond. We found, on reaching the post, that between two and three thousand Indians were assembled, chiefly Potawatomies, Ottawas and Chippewas. Many arrived on the two following days. Provisions were daily issued by the Indian Department during the treaty, to about three thousand."

Chapter 6: Indian Removal From Archer Road

The subject of Indian removal from the states east of the Mississippi quickened in interest when Andrew Jackson made it a presidential campaigning issues. He was elected in 1829, and one of the first measures he urged following his inauguration became known as the "Indian Removal Bill." After one of the bitterest debates in the history of Congress, the bill was enacted into law on May 28, 1830. It did not itself authorize the enforced removal of the Indians, but it announced a federal policy favorable to removal, and placed in the hands of the President the means to initiate steps to secure the removal of any tribe. After enactment of the Removal Bill, commissioners were sent among the tribes to negotiate treaties with them. During the next five years, seventeen more treaties were made to secure cession of the remaining Potawatomies land, and their removal west of the Mississippi River. To vacate the local Potawatomies along the Archer trail, came their special agent, Colonel A.D. Pepper. He arrived in Chicago in August 1833, to attempt organizing their emigration. For weeks the trail was crowded with Indians, who gave themselves up to feasting and dancing. Companies of old warriors could be seen sitting under every hush, smoking, palavering and pow-wowing with great earnest. Besides the chiefs and warriors, there were thousands of other Indians present. Since food was furnished by the government, it attracted all kinds of parasites. Horse traders and horse thieves; rogues of every description, white, black and red; sharpers of every degree; peddlers and grog sellers; Indian agents and commissioners; and contractors to supply the Indians with food, were all there.

The local Potawatomies were encamped on all sides of the wide level prairie beyond Chicago. Many groups were bivouacked on the banks of the Chicago River, and beneath the shelter of low woods, know to have existed a short distance from Lake Michigan along the Archer trail and the South Fork of the Chicago River. Another nearby grove was situated on the Archer trail at the present intersection of Pershing Road and Rockwell Street, and later acquired the name, McKenna's Woods. Finally, on September 26th, 1833, the treaty was formally entered into with the "United Nation of Chippewas, Ottawas and Potawatomies", by which they ceded to the United States their last holdings in Illinois. In addition to alarms paid, agricultural implements, goods and provisions, annuities for twenty years, monies for education, and smaller cash allotments, the Indians were provided with a tract of five million acres on the northeaster side of the Missouri River. The land was approximately one hundred miles wide, extending from the northern to the southern boundary of Iowa. By the treaty, the local Potawatomies along the Archer trail agreed to move to their new reservations within three years, but still they could not bring themselves to abandon their homes at Summit, Palos, the Sag Outlet and Joliet. In the spring of 1836, another few hundred of them were induced to move westward. During two similar operations that followed, in September 1827, and in July 1838, two small groups of Potawatomies were asked to rendezvous at the Desplaines River, adjoining the improved Archer Road. The site was selected by the government officials in order to get the Indians away from the influence of Chicago traders and whiskey sellers. Their last trek westward started July 15, 1838, representing the last organized Potawatomies to be seen along Archer Road.

Chapter 7: Hickory Creek

The thirty mile length of early Archer Road became a thriving commercial thoroughfare landing to the city, nurtured by a number of important arterial roads branching from it from outlying settlements. The major junctions along its route were; south Western Avenue, south Harlem Avenue, route 171 at Summit Crossing the Desplaines river, south LaGrange road, and Archer Road beyond Lockport. One of the earliest settlements at the end of one of these arterial routes to establish trade with Chicago was Hickory Creek, some thirty miles southwest of the city. For generations preceding the white man, Indians found Hickory Creek, a tributary of the Desplaines River to their liking. They favored the hickory wood found there for making bows and arrows. It was no isolated Indian camp instead, it was at the crossroads of the Illinois waterway with the Sauk trail, the latter made popular by the red man who traveled from the Mississippi, thru Detroit, to Canada for their compensation from their early British allies. With some semblance of military protection against the Indians, new settlers from southern Illinois, Indiana and Ohio, migrated into northern Illinois, and a number of them established their homesteads along Hickory Creek, approximately forty allies east of present Joliet, and extending something like fourteen miles along its course. Here they found one of the finest bodies of timber in the state, having an average width along the stream of one mile. Within a short time, productive Hickory Creek turned to Chicago, with its abundant livestock and lumber.

The earliest recorded commercial transaction for livestock at the settlement took place in 1827, when Archibald Clyborne of Chicago, purchased cattle there, as intended provisions for the Fort Dearborn garrison. Like many others that followed, they were led from Hickory Creek over roads that branched into LaGrange Road and Archer Road. It is difficult to preclude the historical importance of this nostalgic settlement by its close proximity to Joliet, as the city grew with the passing of years and Hickory Creek passed into oblivion. William Rice was one of the earliest to settle along its winding course, reportedly in 1827. Two years later he was followed by Aaron Friend, Joseph Norman and Colonel Sayre. Judge John Davison, John Gougar and Lewis Karchival came in 1831, followed the next year by Abraham Francis and John McGavney. Excerps taken from the recorded reminiscence of two pioneers, John Gaugar and Charles Holden, gave a vivid description of early Hickory Creek. "Then there came the late Major Robert A. Kinzie and his family who brought with them very valuable improvement, large quantities of blooded stock, including horses, cattle, and hogs. Hickory Creek was a well behaved stream, it never failed to furnish abundant water for the cattle of farmers, it furnished water for the mills, and well stocked with fish of the pickerel and pike species of bullheads and catfish. The creek run in a southeasterly and northwesterly direction. We found very many Indian items, having but just abandoned the game. There were wigwams, wolf traps, deer runs, etc. The early settlers had hugged the timber belt, and about one settler in ten or a dozen, wanted a mill. It will be observed that there were six saw and grist mills in full operation on Hickory Creek, between the then village of Joliet and Skinners Grove. These mills had been erected prior to 1836, and some o them as early as 1832." An early review of Chicago's commerce read; "The expert trade is stated to consist almost exclusively in produce raised in the surrounding country, and conveyed to the market by the producers in wagons." The foremost commodity at that time was wheat, Chicago affording the only market for Hickory

Creek's grist mills, reached most directly by LaGrange Road and Archer Road.

Chapter 8: Poor Hotel Accommodations

Shortly after settling on Hickory Creek in 1830, John Gougar made a trip to early Chicago, and more than likely traveled to and from his destination over the Archer trail. In his memoirs he wrote; "There were no other inhabitants this side of Chicago. That city was only a trading post. I could not even get a bed in Chicago. A Frenchman, Mark Beaubien, used to come down from there to this trading post. The two men with me got a place with him, but I could not get no bed. We had run out of flour. We went there to get some at Fort Dearborn. It stormed and blew terribly, and we stayed there all day. We started at noon for home. We were two nights and one day coming. We drove fifteen miles, stopped and started a fire. We couldn't lie down because it was too wet. We walked all night in a circle. There came another storm, and it took us all next day to get home. We had lunch just before we left Mark Beaubien, and did not get anything else to eat until we got home. Besides the trading post there were a few other log houses in Chicago." How many times Mark Beaubien traveled over the Archer trail to reach Gougar's Hickory Creek, will never be known. He was a colorful personality whose adventurous activities during the pioneering days of Chicago have been recorded for posterity. Gougars inconvenience, in failing to acquire a bed, took place at Mark Beaubien's famous Sagansh hotel, opening in 1827, on the lot now called the southwest corner of Lake Street and Wacker Drive. Mark's brother, Jean, came to live in Chicago in 1819, when the American Fr Company, worried because rivals were cutting into its trade, sent him there to remedy matters. A few years later, twenty-six year old Mark visited his brother, and decided to make his home on the Chicago River too. He brought his family from Detroit, and put up a log cabin at the southeast side of the Forks, to be designated in later years on Lake and Market Streets, and now on Wacker Drive. He took out a license to run a tavern and got permission to operate a ferry, with the provision that he transport free any citizen of the county. A few years later, Mark built his Saganash hotel across the street, a wooden structure with clapboard sides, on the familiar plan of a central hall with rooms on each side, and had a second story. This building, where in 1830 John Gougar failed to get a bed, remains famous in Chicago history, as one of the substantial inns of stage coach days, often accommodating travelers passing over Archer Road.

The Beaubiens were a light hearted, life loving pair of French Canadians. Mark had a fiddle, and later Jean possessed the first plane. By an assortment of marriages, Mark was the father of twenty-three children, and Jean, the father of nineteen. Mark was described as "a tall, athletic, fine appearing man, French and very polite, opened hearted, generous to a fault, and in his glory at horse race." He did not run his hotel after 1834, when he sold it to John Murphy, and from then on, he kept moving restlessly between Chicago, Peoria, and other towns, apparently no longer interested in starting new enterprises.

The memoirs of John Gougar early visits to Chicago revealed still another noted personality who was familiar with the Archer trail to reach Hickory Creek. He wrote; "The Indians were not troublesome at all. They were more honest than the whites. Shabbona used to be there at times. Shabbona and another man had been to Washington. They had a large wagon and a span of horses. I don't know what their business was in Washington. Shabbona never said much, only when you asked him. The last time I saw him was in Joliet. I did not speak to him then, as he was on the train, and the cars moved off, just as I was about to step on the platform, but I bowed and he recognized me. Shabbona stayed at my house several times. He would refuse a bed and would roll himself in a blanket and sleep on the floor, preferring that, as was his custom." Shabbona, the Potawatomie chief is as close to Chicago's history, as any person who had a part in its beginning. He was the son of an Ottawa chief, born near the Maumee River in Ohio about 1775. Shabbona married a daughter of a Potawatomie chief near Ottawa on the Illinois River, and when his father-in-law died, he became chief of the band. Shortly after that, he removed the village to Shabbona Grove, some sixty miles from Chicago, and about fifteen miles from DeKalb. In 1807 he became associated with Billy Campbell, better known as Saganash, and with Tecumseh, fighting against the Americans and on more than one occasion he risked his life to save those of his white friends. In the Winnebago uprisings in 1927, it was suspected that Big Foot, chief of the Potawatomie at Lake Geneva, would go on the warpath, and Shabbona and Saganash volunteered to go to the village and learn of the plans of action.

Nearing the village they agreed that Shabbona should enter alone, Caldwell remaining outside in hiding to await developments, as they were not at all certain of a friendly reception. At first he was accused of being a spy and was held prisoner all night. He was freed when he expressed indignation that he had come as an ally to counsel with them in their planned war. Shabbona was permitted to return in the company of one of Big Foot's braves. When he was near our shot of Caldwell's concealment he talked loud enough for his partner to understand that he was to set off alone by another route. Once home they warned the white settlers and kept their tribes neutral, discouraging Big Foot from going on the warpath. Again, during the Black Hawk War he sent scouts to warn settlers to flee for the safety of Fort Dearborn. In 1829, he was awarded two sections of land at Shabbona, his village, on which he lived for several years after his tribe was removed to their reservation. When the government notified him in 1837, that all his band, with the exception of his own family must remove to the reservation in western Missouri, he resolved to go with them. Unfortunately for him the Sacs and Foxes had their reservations in close proximity and made attempts on his life in revenge. He returned to Illinois a year later and lived in his grove in peace and quiet until 1849. His Potawatomie friends had been moved to Kansas, when he visited them for three years. When he returned home he found his land in the hands of strangers, having been sold by the United States Land Department, which claimed that his rights were voided by his extended absence. When the old chief fully realized this, he wept like a child. A few friends, seeing the desperate situation of the old chief and his family, purchased him twenty acres of timberland on the Macon River, south of Morris, Illinois, and built a cabin for him. Here he lived with part of his family in semi-poverty. In later years, he seems to have become a victim of drink. The last time he was seen in Chicago was in 1856, four years before he died. Shabbona lies buried in Morris, Illinois. For many years his grave was forgotten and unmarked, but some years ago a stone marker was placed on the last resting place of the chief familiar with the Archer Indian trail.

Chapter 9: The Widow Brown's Road

Early in 1832, the first half of the Archer trail and LaGrange Road, leading to Hickory Creek, were integrated as Cook County's new highway called the Widow Brown's Road. When Cook County was organized in 1831, its original size included present Will, Kane, DuPage, McHenry, Lake and Iroquois counties. The new board formed three voting precincts that were designated as Chicago, Hickory Creek and DuPage. One month later the county made provisions for marking out the first two highways, connecting the districts they had created. These early settlers were appointed as viewers to select the most suitable routes. They were Russell K. Heacock, James Kinzie and Archibald Clybourne. Their original highway report was not only rejected, but they were not compensated for the services. Then in June 1838, Heacock and two new viewers, Elijah Wentworth and Timothy B. Clark, were renamed to select the two highway routes. The second report, recommending two established Indian trails, was approved by the commissioners, and became today's Ogden Avenue, and the east portion of the present Archer Road. The commissioners had decreed that the latter "to run the nearest and best way to the house of Widow Brown at Hickory Creek." Ever since, historians have assumed that the Widow Brown's Pond and the full length of present Archer Road to Lockport, as being the one and same route. This is contrary to a wealth of evidence indicating that today's Archer Road was not "the nearest and best way to the house of Widow Brown." The west segment of Archer Road just beyond the LaGrange Road junction passed through the swamps at the Sag Outlet, an impasse conquered later by Colonel William Archer, when he built a "canal road" through difficult terrain to

Lockport, which he called the Sagannshakee Road, and became the west half of present Archer Road. Joliet was not only a roundabout route to Hickory Creek, at what junction did the Widow Brown's Road separate from the former to reach the southwest settlement? Only one other early Indian trail can be given serious consideration. Today we call it LaGrange Road or 96th Avenue. Historian Scharf called it the Sauganash trail, as it branched southward below the Sagannshakee swamps at the Sag Outlet, and ended a short distance south of present Orland Park. There it interacted with another Indian trail, that ran a corresponding course of today's Southwest Highway, lending to the vicinity of not only Joliet and Lockport, but the "nearest and best way to the house of Widow Brown at Hickory Creek."

The history surrounding the house of Widow Brown, has been buried by the sands of time. It is known that her husband, Joseph Brown and his partner, Aaron Friend, came from the Wabash Valley in 1829. Joseph Brown died in the autumn of 1830, and nothing is known of his wife's activities thereafter, other than the distinction of naming the new Cook County highway after her. In "John Gougar's Early Experiences In Illinois", he stated in a rambling manner; "When I came on September 10, 1830, there were here only Brown, who died in the Fall. Friend, who kept the trading post just above here about a half mile. I have remained here ever since. Davidson came in October sometimes. He brought out Brown." From Gougar's last statement, the supposition would be that after a brief stay the Widow Brown moved away. The presence of deceased kin of the Brown family of later years, buried in the small countryside cemetery on Gougar Road in Hickory Creek, makes it more evident that John Gougar referred to a Brown claim being sold, and not their place of residence.

In an adventurous mood, I paid the fourth generation of Gougars, a visit one summer morning, approaching their farm over the Lincoln Highway, at the junction with Gougars Road. Immediately across the Rock Island tracks, stood the Gougar's house and barn, built in 1840. After introducing myself and explaining the purpose of my visit, I fell under the spell of their captivating hospitality. They proudly showed me genealogical records, dating back to their German ancestry in 1718. Among their collection was a 400 year old German bible with wood binders. They possessed the skull of an Indian chief with all his gear, found in an Indian mound, a short distance from the house, on the south bank of Hickory Creek. I was shown an account book, dated 1836 thru 1840, of William Gougar's general store with records of sales, of such commodities as flour, corn cloth, farm tools and whiskey. The collection of pioneer and Indian relics are worthy of museum protection.

One member of the family, Mr. William Allen, was a most gracious host, in accompanying me on a tour in the vicinity, pointing out the historical landmarks. We walked into the dense Higinsbothan Woods to find the marker placed there by the Will County Centennial Committee, that read; "Site of the Old French Fort, supposedly Erected About 1730." We drove northeast to a farm site approximately a mile and a quarter from the Gougar's farm, and introduced ourselves to its owner, Adolph Chervins. During our conversation, Mr. Allen and I concluded that Mr. Charvin's home was the historical site of the "house of Widow Brown. When we first arrived, Mr. Allen asked Mr. Charvins to be shown the elegant wood paneled carvings that he remembered from his boyhood, had adorned the interior of the enormous barn. He wanted me to see further evidence that we had found the nostalgic terminus at Hickory Creek by viewing the remnants of an old stage coach barn. Regrettingly, Mr. Chervins informed us that he had recently disposed of them. Both of my new acquaintances informed me that at some time they had been told that the house and adjoining barn was once a popular stage coach station between Chicago and St. Louis Mr. Chervins added, that his property abstract did include the name Brown, and when he first came into possession of the house, the window in one room had bars on it, reminiscent of a stage office in the days of Wells Fargo. We concluded our visit, convinced that the farm house on Clinton Road, near the junction with Francis Road in New Lenox, was the former house of Widow Brown.

Continuing our tour of the countryside, we drove north on Gougar Road, stopping a short time later to examine a large stone marker at a road junction which read, "In Memory of John Lane, Who Made The First Steel Plow in 1833 On This Farm." At this point I turned the car around, with the intention of returning Mr. Allen to his home and ending my visit of Hickory Creek. A short distance from our destination, we came upon a small cemetery on the west side of Gougar Road, when Mr. Allen suggested that we stop and examine the names and dates on the tombstones, which might reveal pioneer families of Hickory Creek. Within minutes we found two of the earliest names associated with the early settlement. Here lay the kin of the Brown and Rice families, dating back to 1850. With that, my visit came to an end late that afternoon, with the satisfaction that I had found the house of Widow Brown, and a greater appreciation of the early Hickory Creek settlement.

Chapter 10: Embarrassing Journey

In 1830, two years before a large portion of the Archer Road was integrated as part of the Widow Brown's Road, a very humorous episode was recorded along its route, and at its termination in Hickory Creek. The incident involved Gholson Kercheval, who not only traveled over this early trail, but a short time later, had the distinction of decreeing it a Cook County highway. For this story we are indebted to Mrs. John N. Kinzie, who recounted it in "Wau-Bun" (Early Days), her recollection of early Chicago days, written many years ago. The early settlers at the Hickory Creek settlement were holding a dance, and in an effort to promote friendly relations, invited some young people from distant Chicago to attend. Those that accepted the invitation were three gay blades; Gholson Kercheval; Medard Beaubien, nephew of Mark; and Robert Kinzie.

When the time came for their departure from Chicago, what they lacked in numbers, they made up for in showmanship and elegance. They shed their usual clothes and dressed for the occasion in the best that could be had. Their boots sparkled, suitable to ride their well groomed and sleek horses, one of which was the cherished possession of an officer at Fort Dearborn. The journey down the Archer trail, and its counterpart, to reach Hickory Creek, took them half day, but it was daylight when they reached their destination. Never had the maidens of Hickory Creek beheld such gallant splendor, and saying that they were overwhelmed is an understatement. Their polished manners and ability to execute the pigeon wing and double shuffle, while the fiddler played, awed the beautiful belles of the ball. The enraptured young ladies looked spellbound, as they danced again and again, with the dazzling visitors, totally ignoring their rustic sweethearts, who were awkward even at a conventional gait.

As the night of rivalry wore on, the local boys grew more sullen, and gradually disappeared from the scene. Dawn came streaking in the sky, as the dance ended, and the three Chicago blades, still flushed with the success of their night's conquest, went to the stable to get their horses for the journey home. When they led their mounts out into the daylight, lo and behold, they hardly recognized their animals. The once proud creatures had been shorn of their flowing manes, and their beautiful tails had been shaved bare. Recovering from their initial shock, the young man's feelings turned to rage, but there was no one within sight with whom they could retaliate. The early morning songs of the birds in the trees fell upon unheeding ears. What would the fallen at home have to say? How would the army officer feel about his once beautiful horse? Did the horses themselves realize how terrible they looked? It was too much for young Kercheval, he who soon was to become a county commissioner. According to Mrs. Kinzie, the distraught young man "set down on a legal and cried outright." Nor was their embarrassment alleviated as they rode down the Archer trail and approached the Chicago settlement. There was no way for them to sneak home unnoticed.

They were seen coming across the treeless flatland, once they cleared the wooded area that followed the South Branch, adjoining Archer Road. The entire population of some forty or fifty persons turned out to welcome them. At first, the townspeople were disbelieving of what they saw. Then followed the inevitable shouts of derisive laughter and mortifying jibes, with only here and there a few expressions of sympathy. It is further recorded that the young expressed no further desire to revisit Hickory Creek. In all fairness to Gholson Kareheval, it should be noted that with the regrowth of hair on his horses tail, his resentment disappeared, to the extent that two years later, as Cook County Commissioner, he voted to build a road to the "house of Widow Brown at Hycory Creek". The spirited Kereheval grew up in stature, organizing the first militia company, of which he was captain, and later became postmaster, then Chicago's representative in the state legislature.

Chapter 11: The Butterfield Trace

When historians recorded the annals of the Vincennes Trail, leading from the fertile Wabash Valley to Chicago, they failed to acknowledge the existence of two other routes from that southern region, which branched into Archer Road, before entering the city. Western Avenue was the one that intercepted the Vincennes Trail at Blue Island and siphoned the Wabash trade from there onto Archer Road. The history of this route is narrated in a later chapter. The other route was an extension from the Widow Brown's Road in Hickory Creek, south to Danville, intercepting the Vincennes Trail there. Thus, thriving Hickory Creek not only transported its own abundant farming products and livestock to Chicago over the east portion of today's Archer Road, it also welded a long forgotten trail leading from the rich Wabash Valley. The revelation that the Widow Brown's Road and the Butterfield Trail were one contiguous route from Chicago to Danville, was found in "Long John" Wentworth's Scrapbook, retained by the Chicago Historical Society. One of the two newspaper articles found, dating back to 1879, was from the Watseka Times. At the time the paper was sponsoring an effort to make the history of Iroquois County more complete, and appealed to old timers to submit information that might be of historical significance.

One of the contributed articles was acknowledged in the newspaper by stating "I believe the following is one of the best sketches we have thus far been able to present. It is from the pen of A.D. Rielmer, Esq. of Onarga." The contributor wrote; "A man named Dan Butterfield, living on Gopher Hill, ten miles north of Danville, removed from there about the year 1832, and located on Hickory Creek, some thirty miles southwest of Chicago. He crossed the north fork of the Vermillion at

Bucknell's Point, and entered this county (Iroquis) three miles west of the present site of Hoopeston. The next point was Pigeon Grove, from thence he came to Spring Creek, and forded it at what was called by the early settlers, "The Gap", which was equidistant between Del Ray and Buckley. Keeping the high ground as much as possible, he followed the general course of the timbers to Plato, crossed Prairie Creek at L'Erable, and next Langham Creek, which was then called "White Woman." The Kankakee was passed at Hawkins, which corresponds to the lower and of Bourbonnais Grove. From there the route taken was to Bloom's Grove, thence to Twelve Hill Grove, then in a more northerly direction to Hickory Creek."

"Here Butterfield settled, but the trail was continued; some say to Cooper's Grove (Tinley Woods), thence to Blue Island, where it intersected Hubbard trail (Vincennes Trail), which others, without denying, that it may have forked at Hickory Creek, are positive that the whole travel did not reach Chicago by way of Blue Island. It is important that the entire trail be definitely and correctly located. From the testimony already obtained, I am convinced that from the Kankakee and onward, at least three or four tracks were open to choice. The travel by Hubbard was simply immense. One person informed me that he had seen four large droves of cattle enroute to Chicago at the same time, and in sight of one another, going by this route. That by the other, though far less, was considerable. The Spring Creek and the Urbana settlers, and people in a due southerly direction, as far south as one hundred miles, did their driving and transporting of merchandise by this highway, and as early as 1840, it became an established route."

Also found in Wentworth's Scrapbook, was a newspaper clipping that substantiated K.S. Rieker's conviction that the Butterfield Trail did not enter Chicago by way of Blue Island, and clarified exactly where it entered Hickory Creek. It came into the early settlement from the south, in line with present LaGrange Road, and most likely continued beyond for another 9 ½ miles to blend into the Widow Brown's Road in Orland Park. From there it continued in the same northerly direction, until it intersected with Archer Road, and by this route entered the city. The newspaper article contained Charles Holden's reminiscence of early Hickory Creek, dating back to 1832, when his father settled in Skunks Grove on the Sauk Trail, adjoining Hickory Creek, fourteen miles east of Joliet. He wrote; "There was a road from Chicago to the Wabash, crossing this trail (Sauk), three miles west of us (Butterfield Trail in line with present LaGrange Road), and the old Hubbard Trail, eleven miles east." This nostalgic route from the Wabash Valley, like others branching into Archer Road, contributed greatly to the letters reputation, as a thriving livestock route lending to Chicago.

Chapter 12: The Blackhawk War

During the Blackhawk War in 1832, Archer Road, and its counterpart, the Widow Brown's Road, was the scene of fleeing refugees, seeking the safety of Fort Dearborn. The frontier was in terror. In their fright the settlers had imagined that chief Black Hawk had a grand alliance that was about to desolate the frontier. Although characterized by cruelty on both sides, the incompetence of the soldiers had a more humorous side. The settlements of Hickory Creek and Palos, so intimate with the early history of Archer Road, recorded both comical and grim episodes during that campaign. As soon as Black Hawk threatened to re-cross the Mississippi River, the militia was called out, and from Washington came the regulars under General Henry Atkinson, an army illuminated by the presence of soon to be famous people. The war brought together such men as Zachary, Taylor, Abraham Lincoln, Jefferson Davis; Robert Anderson, of Fort Sumter fame; General Winfield Scott, who rose to the command of the army; General Johnson, of Confederate renown; and Colonel William Beatty Archer, for whom Archer Road was named.

On the sixth of April 1838, Black Hawk re-crossed the Mississippi River, in violation of his treaty. With him came some five hundred warriors and squaws and children, some two thousand in all. Most of them were Sauks, prepared to reoccupy the old land they once possessed. They were determined not to begin hostilities, and Black Hawk sent a series of messages to Atkinson, declaring that his only intention was to make corn, and if the white man wanted to fight, they would have to attack him. That was precisely what occurred. About the middle of May, Major Stillman, at the head of 270 men, advanced toward the Sauk camp, and as he approached, Black Hawk sent out three warriors with a truce flag. The response was brutal. Stillman took the three braves prisoners, and when five more were sent to look for them, the regulars set upon them and killed two. Now the war was on, as Sauks and Foxes began their depredations, pillaging and burning homes, as they killed and captured scattered settlers.

During the uprising, Hickory Creek became the scene of a more humorous incident, reminiscently narrated by pioneer John Gougar, who wrote; "I remember Fort Nonsense. It was Fort Nonsense sure enough. The Indians used to call General Atkinson, who built it, "the Snail", he was so slow. We had a block house here, built in the Sauk War. It was about three-eights of a mile east of here, near the spring. Soldiers were stationed there. Davison, after he came, moved it down to his place for a horse stable." None traveled slowly in those days, but the Indian runners, fleet of foot, brought their own messages to the local Potawatomies, living in the villages on and adjoining the Archer trail, urging them to make trouble among the nearby settlers. Most fortunately, many were friends of the settlers and warned them to flee to the safety of Fort Dearborn. One such ally known along the Archer trail was an Indian called Waupanoosa, who twice came to the Ritchey family in the Palos region, warning them of the threatening danger. On his third visit, when he found his warnings had been disregarded, he explained in disgust, "Jim, fool, no take squaw, papoose fort!" This seemed to have the right effect, for Jim gathered his family together at once and started down Archer Road for Fort Dearborn. One of Ritchey's camping places along the way was besides what is now called Bush's Slough, on 151st Street.

A more serious incident was experienced by Aaron Friend, often mentioned as the partner of Widow Brown's husband, who died in the fall of 1829, shortly after both families settled at

Hickory Creek. This story is attributed to Mrs. Henry Munch of Palos Township, the great granddaughter of Mr. Friend. According to her account, Aaron Friend and his son Charles, sent members of the family from the settlement to Fort Dearborn over the Widow Brown's Road. Father and son lingered to take care of the stock and drops, and were captured by the Indians. During the second night of their capture, as the two men lay with hands and feet strapped to the ground with buckskin thongs. The rain came, wetting the bends and stretching them so that the young men freed one hand and thus untied the knots that bound himself and his father. The older man was weak with buckshots, but although wounded, the two men succeeded in reaching a gun and leaving, they made their way along the Archer trail, subsisting upon wild berries and roots, until at last they came into the fort, hungry ragged and weak from exposure. Mrs. Henry Munch treasures a dream pitcher that her great-grandmother, Friend, used in Fort Dearborn and brought home with her when hostilities had ceased.

The Black Hawk campaign was marked by many episodes of incompetence on the part of the soldiers that included the name of the lamented Abe Lincoln. He was one of the men who responded with sixty-eight men from New Salem, who fell in behind him as their choice of captain. Lincoln knew no military tactics. At one time he was marching with a front of over twenty men across a field, when he wished to pass through a gateway into the next field. As he couldn't remember the word of command, he shouted; "This company is dismissed for two minutes, when it will fall in again on the other side of the gate." On another occasion he led his men across the Henderson River at the cost of wet clothing. Another time, contrary to others, both Lincoln and his men fired off their guns, and as a result, he was compelled to wear a wooden sword.

Sometime later, unknown to Lincoln, his men got hold of some whiskey, and were unable to respond to the order to march the next morning. Again, he was compelled to wear the sword for two days.

But Captain Abraham Lincoln's Company of the First Regiment of the Brigade of Mounted Volunteers, which in the beginning had no horses to mount, never came to combat. It marched and countermarched across Illinois, part of an army of 1600 men under Colonel Zachary Taylor, never catching up with the war, except to bury five men killed in a skirmish. That was real enough, and most of the men no doubt thought it was close enough. Each of the dead, Lincoln remarked, "had a round spot on the top of his head about as big as a dollar, where the redskins had taken his scalp." Even with many shortcomings, the soldiers forced Black Hawk to retreat away from Illinois, across the swamps, forests, prairies and rivers to southern Wisconsin. He was defeated decisively at the Mississippi, near the mouth of the Bad Axe River, but escaped to the Winnebago Village at Prairie LaCross. Deciding to surrender, Black Hawk and his two sons went to Prairie du Chien on August 27, 1832, where they were placed in chains by General Street and Lieutenant Jefferson Davis. President Andrew Jackson was undecided what to do with them, so he had the Indians confined in Fortress Monroe, but on June 4th 1833, they were freed. Although the last of the red men were not removed from the area until 1836, the Black Hawk campaign was the last Indian war endangering the white settlers established along the Archer trail.

Chapter 13: Proposing a Canal

Without any exaggeration, early Archer Road shared in the history of one of the most important routes of North American. Its thirty miles paralleled the most ancient thoroughfare out of Chicago, to white man's knowledge, carrying the heaviest volume of travel. More than chance led the first white man who ever explored the upper Mississippi Valley to the site of the future of Chicago. In the primitive state of the country, the waterway adjoining the Archer trail, possessed an importance unknown to the present generation. The Chicago-Illinois river route constituted one of the natural thoroughfares lending from the St. Lawrence system to the Mississippi River, crowning the Chicago Portage, as one of the five great "keys of the continent." The conditions of travel between Chicago and the southwestern points by water were determined at first by the geographical conditions affecting the Chicago Portage, of carrying small boats or canoes between the navigable Chicago River and the Illinois.

At certain times in the spring, when the rivers were flooded by the melting snow, boats could pass without interruption between these two points. But during much of the year they portaged around the perimeter of the muck-filled slough called Mud Lake that extended from Damen to Harlem Avenue. The trail skirting the north side becomes today's Ogden Avenue, and the Archer trail followed the Southern edge to Summit, acquiring the name "the Desplaines River Canoe trail." At times during extremely dry seasons the earliest travelers were forced to portage as far as the mouth of the Vermillion, a distance of one hundred miles. Further Marquette and Louis Joliet realized the advantage of a short canal, linking the

Chicago with the Desplaines River, and brought the proposal to the attention of their French government. Marquette's journal of the voyage has been preserved, but Joliet lost all his records before he reached his destination. Verbally he gave his report, which included the following suggestion for a canal from the Lakes to the Gulf... "If a channel were out through this ridge (at Kedzie Avenue) one could sail from Lake Illinois to the Sea of Florida." Robert Cavalier LaSalle, visiting the portage in 1682, concluded that a longer canal would be necessary to navigate to the mouth of the Illinois River.

The need for the canal adjoining the adjoining the Archer trail was not seriously considered again, until a century and a quarter later, after the French and British had relinquished the region to the infant American government. One of the earliest problems of the new country was the lack of the adequate facilities for cheap transportation between the interior and our eastern seaboard. When our exporting was still small and embarrassing in foreign trade, goods in any quantity could not be moved down the Mississippi to New Orleans, then to the eastern seaboard, because of the great distance and expense. Thus the cost of exporting and importing in the interior created remote settlements with their own self sufficing economy, such as Chicago had with early Hickory Creek and the Wabash Valley. As part of a national effort to relieve the economic burdens of transportation, the Illinois and Michigan canal was suggested by Peter H. Porter of New York in 1810, but to no avail. The unfortunate experiences of the second war with Great Britain in 1818, emphasized the importance of such a route over which military and naval forces and supplies could be transported to the north Canadian frontier. The first practical step was taken August 24, 1816, by the treaty with the Indiana, removing them from a strip of land along the route of the suggested waterway. As a further step in the same direction, two successive examinations of the physical character of the region was made by the War Department, both agreeing to the importance, ease and relatively small expense in constructing a canal adjoining the Archer trail. The first report was made by Major Stephan H. Long, March 4, 1817, and the other by R. Graham and Joseph Phillips on April 4, 1819. Their plans were fatally smitten by President Monroe's indifference and that of the South, as well as by the hostility of the West. The latter did not favor any internal improvements, which would result in further migration from the North Atlantic seaboard. At this stage of the development of the project, local interest began to play a part. It was on the same day on which the House of Representatives passed a resolution that Secretary of War, John C. Calhoun, report a plan for system of military roads and canals, and that the bill for the admission of Illinois into the Union was so amended, as to move its northern boundary from the bottom of Lake Michigan to the present border at Wisconsin, a distance of forty-one miles. This placed the port of Chicago within the boundaries of the newly created state of Illinois in 1818. During the Second General Assembly, the question of the canal was taken up with the federal government with vigor.

Daniel Pope Cook, for whom Cook County has been normal sitting in the House of Representatives, and with Jesse B. Thomas in the Senate, succeeded March 30, 1822, in acquiring a strip of land on which the canal should stand. They gained an added ninety feet on each side of it, but acquired no financial aid from the federal government for its construction. The General Assembly of Illinois, by the Act of February 14, 1823, appointed a board of commissioners to determine the most available route for the canal, and to estimate its cost for construction. In the autumn of 1823, an examination of the region was made, but no accounts survey was completed until the following year. Five routes were surveyed over the same general course, adjoining the Archer trail from the South Branch of the Chicago River to the Desplaines Valley, and down to the Illinois River. The estimated cost varied for the different routes, from $639,542.78 to $716,110.71. After the canal's completion in 1848, engineers estimated the actual cost of the Illinois and Michigan canal at $8,654,337.51.

The John Quincy Adams administration assumed a more liberal attitude toward the internal improvement, and on March 2, 1827, the federal government donated to the state of Illinois, for the purpose of aiding the construction of the canal, the alternate section of land for a distance of five miles on each side of the proposed waterway. Under the Act of January 22, 1829, a new canal commission was appointed to take charge of the work of raising the necessary funds and placing the work in process of construction. Under the direction of this commission, land sales were begun, the towns of Ottawa and Chicago were laid out, town lots were sold, and new plans and estimates for the work was prepared. The land sales proved disappointing because men hesitated to invest in canal lands, till convinced that the construction of the canal would not be further delayed. Meanwhile a new menace to the canal project had arisen by the beginning of 1831, with the idea that the railroad was destined as the future mode of transportation. When Governor Reynolds changed his support from the canal for the railroad, in a speech made December 4, 1832, the General Assembly followed, by advocating the same on January 7, 1853. Unable to settle the vexing question, the canal commission was abolished and left the state without either the canal or railroad.

Chapter 14: Constructing the Waterway

The tread migration and the growing need for better commercial relations between Chicago and the growing southwest settlements along the Illinois waterway became more imperative for such places as Ottawa, Peru and Peoria. Many came by way of the Archer trail, some using that segment between Chicago and Summit, crossing the Desplaines at this point to follow the Joliet trail on the north bank of the river. Others continued on Archer trail's counterpart, the Widow Brown's Road, passing through Hickory Creek and then Joliet, to reach their destination along the Illinois River.

Steamboats were plying on the Illinois River as far up as Peoria, and could readily extend their operations to LaSalle, the western terminus of the proposed canal. In spite of the comparatively heavy cost of transporting merchandise by wagon across the country from Chicago, this route was cheaper than the river and ocean route by way of New Orleans. The agitation for the canal became a political campaign in 1834, and men were chosen to the General Assembly entirely on the basis of their known attitude toward the question of the canal. Joseph Duncan, an intimate friend of Colonel William Beatty Archer, was a staunch supporter of the canal, and was elected Governor. An Act of February 10, 1835, provided for the appointment of the third canal commission. They were General William F. Thornton, Colonel Gurdon S. Hubbard, and Colonel William Archer.

The reorganization set of January 9, 1836, pledged the credit and faith of the statue to the payment of loans, and every effort to get the canal underway at the earliest possible moment was made, believing that the more activity the easier would be the task of financing it. Colonel Archer was the acting commissioner, which is reality was the same as field superintendent. The work was laid out in three divisions, known as the Summit, the Middle, and the Western divisions.

Deeming it good policy to begin operations in the vanity of Chicago, a seven mile portion of the Summit division, from the Chicago River at Ashland Avenue to the "Point of Oaks", near Harlem Avenue, was undertaken. The work of constructing the canal was formerly begun with imposing ceremonies, and a great celebration at 2900 South Ashland Avenue, adjoining the Archer trail, on July 4, 1836. The first shovel of earth was turned over by Colonel William Beatty Archer. Not much progress was made during the summer and autumn, and much of the time was consumed in preliminary preparations, such as constructing and grading a canal road that was to be named the Archer Road, leading to the newly plotted canal town of Lockport.

Chapter 15: The Saganashkee Road

In his capacity as acting commissioner, Colonel Archer was criticized for establishing the town of Lockport in such alone proximity with Joliet, four miles away, and for changing the thirty mile length of the Archer Indian trail into a "canal road", at an expense of $40,000 for the purpose of connecting Chicago with his newly plotted town. Historian Andreas implied that Colonel Archer had much to gain by building the new town and road, supposedly because he had extensive holdings there. That possibility was remote, for the Colonel was the life and breadth of the town of Marshall, 190 miles south of Chicago, which he had founded the year before, spending a lifetime there, as compared to approximately two years in this area as canal commissioner.

Even before Colonel Archer improved the Archer trail, Indians traversed over this legendary route, passing through the marshes that lay between their large villages at the Sag Outlet and Joliet. But the white settlers, with their wagons and live stock drives, avoided both the swamps and Sag Indian village, by turning south over LaGrange Road, an integrated part of the Widow Brown's Road, leading to Hickory Creek and Joliet. Archer's major accomplishment was in grading and bridging these swamps from the Sag Outlet to Lockport, which in his biographical papers he referred to as "improving the Saganashkee Road." With its completion, the east fifteen miles from Chicago to LaGrange Road was joined with the fifteen mile length of the Saganashkee Road to Lockport, creating the thirty mile long Archer Road of today.

The origins of the name, Saganashkee, can be attributed to Jesse W. Weik, who became an intimate friend of Major James

M. Bucklin, during the letters advanced years of retirement in Greencastle, Indiana. Mr. Weik recorded Major Bucklin's reminiscence as chief engineer during 1831, when he laid out the course of the Illinois and Michigan canal. Excerpts taken from Mr. Weik's article, appeared in the 1917 Illinois State Historical Journal, quoting the Major as saying; "From the ford of the Ausoganashkee, or Reed Swamp (often abbreviated to the Sauganash or Sag) the excavation was sixteen feet deep, the six feet consisting of sand and clay, and the remaining ten feet of limestone." Thus before his death on April 12, 1890, Major Bucklin revealed that the Indians called the region around the Sag Outlet, Ausoganashkee, meaning reed swamp. Such later derivations from the original name became; Saganashkee, Sag and Gaunashke, a result of white man's continued corruption in spelling Indian names. Historian Scharf called the adjoining swamps of Palos, Gau-nash-ke, and some years later the canal built through these swamps to feed the Illinois and Michigan Canal, was named the Sag canal. To our present day, the Cook County Forest Preserves has perpetuated Colonel Archer's perverted spelling, by calling an enclosed body of water, adjoining both canals, the Saganashkee Slough.

Chapter 16: Lockport

As Archer Road ends and State Street begins, you enter nostalgic Lockport, with its many modern oil refineries and homes, and historical edifices, reminiscent of the canal era that created the town many years ago. The picturesque Illinois & Michigan canal office still stands on the main thoroughfare, its function reduced to leasing the ninety feet granted by the Federal government to the state of Illinois back in 1827. Across the street is the Lockport library, which possesses a small brochure, written by its citizens, poetically summarizing the origin of the Town's history. The introduction reads; "Through this settlement ran an age old Indian trail. Across this, countless generations of Potawatomies had drifted to and from between the Illinois River. This trail was probably followed to some extent by Colonel Archer, who surveyed the route of the highway, which was to take his name." The first semblance of homesteading in the vicinity of Lockport took place in October 1830, when a man with his wife and children came and settled near a brook, just north of the present town. Within a few months, others came, and in a year or so, there was a settlement of possibly a half dozen families. When the present town was platted in 1836 by a surveyor named Wampler, and supervised by Colonel Archer, the adjoining settlement had grown to a village called Runyontown", named for the founder, Armstead Runyon. As years passed they were integrated into the new town of Lockport.

Shortly after Colonel Archer completed the "canal road", and started digging the adjoining waterway, the scarcity of laborers along the canal line seriously retarded the progress of the work. It placed him and the other commissioners under fire.

They were criticized for underestimating the canal cost and omitting entirely several important items of expense, such as the $40,000 in constructing Archer Road. The result of the attack was the reorganization of the canal board, transferring the power of appointments from Colonel Archer's intimate friend, Governor Duncan, to the General Assembly. At this point, William Archer and Gurdon Hubbard were not reappointed, and the new board formed consisted of incumbent General William F. Thornton, General Jacob Fry, and Colonel J. A. McClernand. Thus ended Colonel Archer's two year association with the construction of the Illinois and Michigan canal that had started February 10, 1835 and ended March 8, 1837. The exact date or act, officially naming Archer Road in his honor is not known.

It took twelve years to complete the canal, and when it opened in 1848, the officials clambered on board the canal boat General Fry, and made the first trip from Lockport to Chicago on April 10th. But a few days later the canal served its real purpose, when the General Thornton passed the length of the canal from LaSalle to Chicago, with a cargo of sugar from New Orleans, bound for Buffalo. The growing revenue of the canal was of short duration, for in 1851, Chicago's first railroad was organized. Lockport, so dependent upon the prosperity of the canal, had its warning of the competition that was to blast its hopes, and bring its submission to adjoining Joliet, with its inherent resources. The early tragedy was summarized in the "History of Will County, Past and Present" by W. W. Stevens, who wrote; "That the town did not become the leading town in the country is no fault of the canal commissioners, for they all did all in their power to make it the leading town in the county, but the leading town on the whole canal. They not only located the principal offices of the canal there, but they built a great road from the offices to Chicago at a cost of $40,000 to the state. After the building of the road, it became the great thoroughfare between the western part of the county and Chicago, and hence all traffic in that direction must necessarily pass through the town." The "History of Will County" by Wm. LaBaron Jr. was more critical of the Lockport project. "The canal commissioners, as well as the many other persons of intelligence, probably overrated the advantages of the locality for a commercial and manufacturing town. Joliet, only four miles to the mouth of the site selected for Lockport, and at that time been laid out and established as the county seat, and the natural advantages of its position, with the agricultural and mining wealth surrounding it, would preclude the existence of other towns in such close proximity."

As a result of the expanding railroads, the canal was abandoned, stifling Lockport's growth. The town's original destiny of controlling the waters between Lake Michigan and the Mississippi, was restored in 1900, with the opening of the new Chicago Sanitary and Ship canal. Lockport, thirty-six miles from the mouth of the Chicago River at Lake Michigan, still maintains two locks, day and night for towboats and barges carrying heavy freight, numbering from 8,000 to 10,000 craft each year. The War Department operates the lock with a forty foot drop, with one gate measuring twenty feet in height, and the other at the opposite and towering sixty feet. The water between them can be lowered in fifteen minutes. The other look is for smaller crafts, operated by the Chicago Sanitary District, accommodating over five hundred boats a year. In addition, the locks help regulate the amount of water drawn from Lake Michigan, and generate electric power for the surrounding area. Lockport's interim, between the two canals era's, has served as an advantage to this picturesque and staid town, reflecting conservative planning, by avoiding encroaching homes, narrow and congested streets, and slums, found in its neighboring boom cities.

Chapter 17: Bridgeport's Archey Road

Long before the completion of the Illinois and Michigan canal in 1848, the Bridgeport settlement at its east terminus, already possessed a substantial segment of Chicago's earliest commercial enterprises. Archer Road, passing through the heart of the community, was the scene of repeated caravans of wheat wagons and livestock drives moving to the early city. The initial slaughter houses were located near the business district, along the North Branch of the Chicago River, until a number of livestock man realized the advantages of establishing them at the south and southwest ends of the city, nearer the trails leading from the thriving Wabash Valley. In 1834, Oliver Newberry and George W. Dole were the first to erect a packing house on the South Branch. During their initial year of operation they packed 300 cattle and 1400 hogs. About the same time the earliest Irish immigrants came and built their shacks and frame houses in Bridgeport, between the South Branch and Archer Road. The packing industry was expanded along the South Branch in 1843, when partners John P. Chapin and Thomas Dyer opened their new establishment, before each had their opportunity to serve as mayor of Chicago. By 1845, Bridgeport became a thriving village, with its Irish digging the Illinois and Michigan canal, or working at the packing houses. Their toll was reflected in the extensive review of Chicago's business in 1846, which read; "The export trade is stated to consist almost exclusively in produce, raised in the surrounding country, and conveyed to the market by the producers in wagons." Much of this early traffic entered the city over Archer Road, which is the mouths of the Bridgeport Irish becomes Archer Road. They found much employment when the foremost commodity was wheat, and Chicago afforded the only market for the farmers beyond in Grundy County and LaSalle, and others even more remote. In 1842, Ottawa alone, advertised for fifty teams to haul wheat to Chicago, many that some by the way of Archer Road through Bridgeport. Along its route, warehouses were erected, and a market for grain of all kinds was brought within easy reach.

Bridgeport, known until this day for its existing livestock enterprises, increased to a feverish pitch with the opening of the Illinois and Michigan canal in 1843. Here at this east terminus, it divided into the bracelets like a "Y", just before the canal came from the west to wheat is now Ashland Avenue. The North Branch was the main canal, and had a lock with gates and abutments of limestone. These gates separated the water of the canal from the South Fork of the Chicago River. The other half of the "Y" the South Branch of the canal ran a short distance east of present Ashland Avenue and stopped short of the South Fork. Here it dead-ended for barges that were loading and unloading goods. The South Branch of the canal was on a line with Bridgeport's Fuller Street, which was laid out in 1856. In the early days of the canal, horses and mules were used to tow barges, and the ground was packed solid by their hoofs all along the route, before the tugboat came into use. There were saloons, boardinghouses, grocery stores and stables, and they took care of the wants of brawny men, teamsters, barge men, tug boat crews and freight handlers.

Biggest of the frame houses was the Canal House that served as the center of early Bridgeport. The activities of his historical edifice brought the city's first omnibus service from the business district to the canal office doors in 1859. Bridgeport become a noisy, brawling village, with mule skinners coming off the tow path; teamsters arriving with heavy loads, unhitching their horses and putting up the Canal House; barges arriving with goods and passengers; Frink & Walker's stage coaches standing by to convey canal passengers down Archey Road to the business district of the city; and livestock being led to the adjoining packing houses. The Canal House was a prosperous inn, always full of boarders, besides a great rash of transient customers. This was the head and end of the packet line on the canal, and right in this immediate vicinity were the stables, where daily were quartered from 300 to 400 mules. Captains of the boats and the crews all made the Canal House their headquarters, and many a wild time were held within its walls. It is said that during the 1840's, Stephen A. Douglas was its guest several times, and once the lamented Lincoln honored its presence. It was a frame structure, three stories high, built in the shape of an "L", fronting on one side along the canal, and only a few feed from Ashland Avenue on the opposite side. More livestock enterprises were erected in Bridgeport, as recorded in the Den of the Prairie, dated November 16, 1860. It read, "R. W. and C. G. Hough are located a short distance below Bridgeport, immediately on the banks of the river (Throop Street). Their buildings are thirty by sixty feet in size with wings. They are working fifty hands and slaughtering one hundred and thirty head of cattle per day. Cash paid for cattle, $70,000; for salt, barrels and labor, $15,000; total $85,000." Their building initially cost them $3,000 and in 1853, they built larger facilities at an expense of $20,000. In 1856, they were completely burned out, but reconstructed their business at a cost of $25,000. Two years before, the Cragin Company of New York also opened a new packing house in Bridgeport, costing $45,000, and operated by their agent, John L. Hancock.

Chapter 18: Lincoln Challenged

When the civil war started in 1861, the political views of the Bridgeport Irish and Colonel Archer were at opposite poles. The early Irish immigrants of the settlement had worked under the supervision of the Colonel, building the Archer Road and digging the canal during his tenure back in 1856-57. In the following year in his home town of Marshall, 190 miles south of Chicago, he was re-elected to the House of Representatives, serving two terms with Abraham Lincoln, which doubtlessly was the commencement of their mutual admiration and friendship. When William Archer was a delegate to the first Republican convention at Philadelphia in 1856, he enthusiastically supported Lincoln's candidacy for the office of vice president. During the convention deliberations, when Archer purposed the name of Lincoln, a part member sarcastically asked, "Who is Lincoln? Can he fight?" The Colonel answered; "Yes, by Guinea, he can and so can I." In a letter written by Archer from Washington D.C. June 21, 1856, to his friend Henry Pelham Holmes Bromwell, at his residence in Charleston, Illinois, he wrote, "I started A. Lincoln for vice president on the evening of the 18th after dark, and it took well."

The die was cast when Bridgeport's idol, Stephen A. Douglas, Chicago's famous senator lost the presidency to Colonel Archer's intimate friend, Abraham Lincoln, with the outbreak of the Civil War, the Irish on Archey Road reacted violently in opposing the president, joined by the equally fervent Democrats from the East, and those from the Old South who had settled in Chicago. The bitterness along Archey road grew against Lincoln, for they felt that after committing their sons to serve the Union, the president had led them into war for the freedom of Negroes. To Lincoln's call for volunteers, the sons of Chicago gave an instant warm response, but down along Archer Road, the Irish laborers threw rocks at Negroes as possible rivals for the jobs. As Catholics, they had been hounded by the Puritan wing of the Republican party. They now took revenge when eve the Tribune was forced by events to print more and more news of Lee's victories. The Irish down along their Archey Road roared cheers in saloons and on the street, while little groups all over the city were secretly jubilant indoors.

Some help came from the gallant enemy, Stephen Douglas. He has upheld the Union all his life and returned to Chicago, calling on the Irish along Archey Road and all his other followers to rally behind President Lincoln. "No one can be a true Democrat without being a patriot!" he declared. The Irish of Bridgeport responded by the formation of Mulligan's brigade. He was captured early in the war, exchanged and returned to battle, and was killed at Winchester, Virginia. Mulligan's bravery has been perpetuated by Chicago streets named in his honor, Winchester Avenue crossing over Archer Road at 1938 West; and Mulligan Avenue at 6532 West.

But a minority of Irish in Bridgeport retained their views against President Lincoln, and the power of their bitterness was multiplied by the repression used against them. Their feelings rose to riot heat in June 1856, when General Burnside, who was in charge of the Chicago region, ordered the suppression of their newspaper, the Times. When his troops from Camp Douglas prison camp at 36th and Cottage Grove Avenue, marched into town and seized the plant, a mob gathered outside and threatened to storm the building of the hated Tribune nearby. The situation was eased when Lincoln sent a telegram which promptly ended that attempt to kill the freedom of the press. So the Times continued to pour out its reports and editorials of Union defeats, of sons, brothers and husbands killed, and of people all over the North who were sick and tired of fighting for the Negroes. They continued to clamor for the time when Johnny could come marching home. So hell broke out once more then in 1864 Lincoln ran for a second term. Democrats gathered in convention in Chicago to nominate a man who stood for ending this useless war by signing up with the South. Hobe paraded shouting war songs as fists were used and bricks were hurled and a member of leaders were jailed. The efficiency of the Chicago police under Democrat Long John Wentworth dispelled the storm, and the next day the convention dropped their fiery candidate. Pause along Archer Road finally came the following April, at war's end with Lee's surrender at Appomattox.

Chapter 19: Undaunted Gaelic Spirit

During the canal era, Bridgeport became a community of distorted streets, lined with wooden shanties. More shacks were built along the north bank of the waterway and because known as the Levee. Naturally the streets acquired such Irish names as Quinn, Kaeley, Bonfield, Haynee, Arch, Farrell, Grady and Oratten, and even the adjoining body of water becomes Healy's slough. A nostalgic newspaper clipping was discovered in John Wentworth's scrapbook, retained by the Chicago Historical Society that made reference to that historical water hole. The article has been sent to the editor of the Inter-Ocean newspaper by an early pioneer, who reminiscently stated; "Coming to Chicago in 1835, and having the love for hunting and fishing, I roamed the prairies in the winding South Branch of the Chicago River. He used to catch them in Mosely's slough, and at the bridge over the "Branch" on Archer Road. I fished at the headwaters of the South Branch for the sake of old times too, and had "first rate" luck. I caught an abundance of "bulponts" about six inches long, as late as September in 1871."

The adulterated spelling of Archer Road to Archey Road by the Bridgeport Irish was perpetuated by the noted author, Finley Peter Dunn, during Chicago's World's Fair in 1895. He humorously illustrated their political interests, saturated with Irish brogues in the colorful "Dooley Stories," When Mr. Dunne's sketches became popular, the conversations of Mr. Doolay, Mr. Hennessey and others, on any worldly subject, really took place in McCarry's saloon, on the spot once covered by the former Boston Department Store on State Street. In his first sketches he called the saloon man, McNary, which disturbed the authentic McCarry to such a boiling point, that

Dunne was forced to make a revision. He knew that there were so many Dooleys and Hennessey on Archey Road that no one could be greatly embarrassed. Thus Dooley the Celebrity was born. And Mr. Hennessey was taken from life, and Archey Roader named John J. McKenna, who in reality, had not been a resident of Bridgeport since the Great Chicago Fire 1871, and thereafter became an outstanding figure in Brighton Park, a mile further west. McKenna, whose detailed accomplishments are narrated in a later chapter, cherishingly saved faded clippings of some of the first Doolay stories that were printed, and in those sketches was quoted by his rightful name. The saloon man McNary jeered the Fair after visiting it with McKenna; "Come on and see the' Midway," he [sez] "That's h— l," he [sez] "So over we go to the Midway, an', Johnny, I haven't been well since."

Long before the period of the Dooley stories, the fortunes of Bridgeport and had greatly changed. The traffic of the Illinois and Michigan canal had been lost to the railroads, and the opening of the Union Stock Yards at 42nd and Halsted Street in 1865, was another blow to the brawling community, reducing the commercial livestock establishments there to a few. By the 1890's, it was cloudy giving up its life. In those forlorn days, George Ado was writing a daily feature about Chicago, "Stories of the Streets and of the Town", for the Chicago Record, and John McCutcheon was illustrating it. They visited the canal site adjoining Archer Road in Bridgeport, which still had sixty banjos plying between Chicago and Illinois River, but was now something of a relic. The Bridgeport pumps were emptying "black water from the yards" into the canal, the mark of decay. The canal House was sagging, leaning wearily on its supports. Its windows had been torn out and the front doors were nailed over with boards. The warped clapboards had been worn black by wind and weather. Nothing was needed to complete its ruin.

A few years before, a man reopened the front room as a saloon, surprising the few old canal boats creeping by to see a new gilt sign on the dingy front. They were not surprised when a short time later, the sign disappeared and the boards were again nailed over the front. The square-fronted building standing vacant along the abandoned canal were nailed with rough boards over doors and windows, and sometimes for half a day at a time, no living thing was seen moving along the deported water front. The greatness of the Canal House and the Levee lives only in memory. The undaunted Gaelic spirit was not to be subdued, as the Irish expanded north of Archer Road, away from the "canal ghost town", reaching Thirty-ninth Street and after Chicago incorporated the village of Bridgeport in 1863. In their midst remained a number of the early companies producing by-products from livestock, led by the renowned Armour Company. The vitality of the Bridgeport Irish emerged more so in the field of public services and politics. The Bridgeport Keeley's gave the city a police chief; Bonafield Street was named for the family of John Bonafield, who was captain of police at the Haymarket riot, the night the bomb was thrown in 1886. Over the years, many of its Irish citizens attained high positions of public trust, contributing to the greatness of the city. The dynamic spirit of the Bridgeport Irish has been perpetuated by Chicago's mayor, Richard J. Daley, whose accomplishments in improving the city has been monumental.

Chapter 20: Town of Brighton

That portion of Archer Road, from Western Avenue (2400 West) to Central Park Avenue (3600 West), passes through Chicago's three square mile residential community of Brighton Park, serving as its main business thoroughfare. Prior to the city's expansive annexations in all directions in 1889, the community was a suburb of Chicago, called the "Town of Brighton." Its early activities possessed all the charm of a frontier saga, never before correlated with the written annals of Chicago's livestock history. For the fact that it once lay outside the city's southwest boundaries, the sands of time had all but hidden its very distinctive history that flourished with the Hoosier cattle drives from "down on the Wabash", attracted to Brighton's thriving stock yards, its drovers hotel and beautiful race track. The unrecorded popularity of the livestock enterprise on Archer Road in Brighton was once known throughout the state, when in 1861, it became the site for the annual Illinois State Fair.

The Town of Brighton came into existence in 1868, when two enterprising Chicago businessmen, John Evans and Nicholas Pinell Iglehart, constructed a hotel and stock yard at the junction of Archer Road and Blue Island Road (Western Avenue), realizing the commercial advantages of adjoining two thriving livestock trails leading into the city. The Blue Island Road was Archer Road's most important counterpart, over which stock were led from Wabash Valley to the stop-over town of Blue Island, twelve miles south of Brighton. From Blue Island they entered the city by two routes; over present Vincennes Avenue, and by way of today's Western Avenue. As they came down the latter, and reached the Archer Road junction, the stock were either diverted northeastward to the packing houses in Bridgeport, or they continued north to Twenty-sixth Street, then turned northeastward over present Blue Island Avenues, to stock yards and packing houses located closer to Chicago's early business district. The full length of this route, from the stop-over town twelve miles to the south, leading into the city, acquired the name of Blue Island Road. It was changed to Western Avenue sometime after 1863, but the diagonal segment from Twenty-sixth Street, northeastward toward downtown, has still retained its original name of Blue Island Avenue.

The co-founders of Brighton, Evans and Iglehart, made two eighty acre purchases at the Archer and Western Avenues junction, in October 1852 and March 1853. Eight months later they sub-divided their holdings into 160, one more lots and called it the "town of Brighton", although they never legally had it incorporated with the state. To assure the continued flow of livestock down Western Avenue to the junction with Archer Road, they and other associates initiated the improvement of the route by making it a plank road, a new and revolutionary innovation at the time. The Blue Island Plank Road Company was formed by Evans and Iglehart, with John McCaffery, "the father of Brighton", General Richard K. Swift, noted Chicago banker, and William Johnson, banking associate. A notice that subscriptions were open for stock for the corporation was published in the Democratic Press in July 1863. The improvement was generally known as the New Plank Road in order to distinguish it from the others, In the Chicago Tribune dated Wednesday, October 19th, 1855, reference to the improvement read; "Blue Island Plank Road", "The work on this important thoroughfare is being pushed forward as fast as men and material can be procured. A large supply of plank has been contracted for, and it is designed to have the Avenue in good traveling order by the opening of Spring. The distance to the town of Worth, from the city limits is about 13 miles, and this route will be the nearest to the city for all travel from the south by that direction. The immense droves of cattle annually driven to this city will without doubt take the Plank Road at Worth, as it is on the direct air line to the new town of Brighton recently laid out just beyond the city limits for a cattle mart."

Another reference to tee plank road appeared in the Democratic Press of November 1853, which read; "After the completion of the New Plank Road to Blue Island, this will be the route of travel to take between this point and the city. The bridges of the plank road across the canal and the West Fork of the Chicago River, are up and nearly ready for crossing. They are a fine substantial structure built in Stone and Boomer's best style. The planks are being laid and spiked on the road beds so rapidly as a strong force of men can put them down. The Avenue will be 120 feet wide, south of the canal to the head of Blue Island."

Chapter 21: Unheralded Stock Yards

As the construction of the Blue Island Plank Road continued, Evans and Iglehart commenced the building of the Brighton drovers hotel and stock yards. The elaborate two-story frame building was erected on the southwest corner of Archer Road and Western Avenue, fronting on the former, surrounded by a beautiful grove of trees. Reference to their work appeared in the Democratic Press dated Saturday, October 28, 1854, which read; "We have been shown the catalogue of the great sale of real estate that comes off next Monday at the office of J.A. Marshall & Co. on Dearborn Street. An examination of the list above that there is a large amount of very excellent property in different parts of the city to be offered. There is also a great many lots of one more each on the list, in the town of Brighton, which is destined to become an important suburban village. The new large and elegant hotel has recently been erected in Brighton, with the most extensive cattle yards in the west (which by the way have for sometime been full of cattle) indicates to some extent the future prospects of this beautiful place, heretofore, a neglected neighborhood has been improved."

The glowing predictions of Brighton's livestocks future were also proclaimed in the annual review of Chicago's commerce by the prominent editorialist, William "Deacon" Bross, who later became president of the Chicago Tribune and Lieutenant-Governor of Illinois. The Blue Island Plank Road was still under construction when he was quoted as saying; "Moreover, as by this road, cattle could e driven to the city without danger of fright from locomotives, and as two of the principal roads entering the city meet at Brighton, with an abundance of water at all times, and pastures and meadow lands in almost unlimited quantities beyond, one can doubt, it's favorable position of becoming the principal cattle market of Chicago." More acclaim for Brighton's early reputation appeared in the Democratic Press of Monday, September 3, 1855, that read; "This little suburb is becoming quite famous as a cattle market. The firm hotel erected by the proprietors of the town, affords a pleasant stopping place for our country friends. The yards are spacious and well arranged, and the best of pasturage can be obtained in the immediate vicinity without the cost of a penny. Within the last two months, large quantities of cattle, sheep and hogs have changed hands at Brighton."

As the beautiful Brighton House was being completed in 1854, colorful "Long John" Wentworth purchased the complete square mile adjoining the Brighton stock yards, through which Archer Road passed diagonally. He sold most of it by 1860, but retained 74.88 acres that became an integral part of the thriving Brighton livestock enterprise. Wentworth also owned an enormous farm "retreat" on Archer Road in Summit, but he was known for his love for the bustling life of the city. Prior to becoming a resident of the Sherman House, until his death in 1868, he lived in the historical Tremont House. During his early residence at the latter, the hotel came into the hands of brothers, George and David Gage in 1863, shortly after their arrival from Boston. Wentworth and the Gage Brothers became friends, which became quite evident in 1855, when the brothers acquired a quarter interest in the distant Brighton House, and opened the beautiful Brighton race track on Wentworth's property, adjoining the hotel and stock yards. The course acquired an early reputation as being "the most luxurious race track west of New York." The Chicago Tribune of Wednesday, June 20, 1855, revealed the date of its opening. The article read; "Trotting Races", "The first trotting races on the new track at Brighton commenced at 3 o'clock yesterday afternoon, and are to be continued for the week. The "fast" men and horses about town will enjoy themselves amazingly. The Brighton House under the auspices of Mr. Winer, is flourishing and full of business, and everything looks neat and new as a pin. The stable and yards are comfortable, and everything looks neat and new as a pin. The stable and yards are comfortable, and the grazing in the vicinity excellent. This is likely to become a favorable market for cattle drovers, and it appears to us might do well enough with the race track attached."

Chapter 22: Notorious Gamblers

By a ruse attributed to Chicago's new mayor of one north, notorious gamblers from the city's vilest district called the Sands, were attracted to the Brighton race track located at the southwest corner of Archer Road and Western Avenue, while he destroyed their home. Major "Long John" Wentworth was known for personally leading such raids on gambling houses, brothels, and any area that was described as a pocket of crime, and once in a fit of anger at the legislature, he fired the entire police department. The biggest and most spectacular raid Wentworth led was against an area north of the Chicago River, toward the lake, a district called the Sands. It was a haven for thieves, pick pockets, gamblers, prostitutes, and others of the underworld. How "Long John" attracted the incorrigibles from their district was revealed in an early newspaper clipping found in John Wentworth's Scrapbook, retained by the Chicago Historical Society. It indicated that the mayor did not have in his command a sufficient force of policemen to successfully invade the district, but he had a brain that was capable of conceiving a plan which would work satisfactorily. In his old Chicago Democratic newspaper plant, he had some hundreds of large bills struck off, announcing that a dog fight for a purse of $500.00 was to behalf at the Brighton track, between the dog of Dutch Frank, a Sands brothel owner, and the hound of William Gallager, a Market Street butcher. The bills were posted throughout the Sands and naturally attracted the attention of the inhabitants. On the morning of April 20, 1857, every able bodied man in the Sands accompanied Dutch Frank to the Brighton track, while Mayor Wentworth mustered thirty police and firemen for his attack on their abandoned district.

They came equipped with iron hooks on the end of tackles, and attached to sturdy teams of horses. As Long John led the assault from his carriage, tackles were hooked to key spots on a dozen or more shacks and huts, and were tumbled down by the straining team of horses. A number of buildings, too sturdy for such an operation were burned to the ground, completely destroying the Sands. Wentworth's colorful escapade has been frequently reviewed by Chicago newspapers and narrated by authors, but no mention has ever been made that Long John actually owned the Brighton race track site on Archer Road, from 1864 to his death in 1888.

Chapter 23: State Fair at Brighton

Four years after Iglehart and Evans opened the Brighton stock yards on Archer Road in 1853, the letter withdrew from the company, as new associates with Iglehart reorganized the business by incorporating the "Brighton Hotel and Stock Yard Company." John Evans, for whom Evanston, Illinois had been named, was known for his outstanding achievements as a civic, business and political leader, educator, religious lecturer, and railroad builder. He finally went on to become Territorial Governor of Colorado, where his outstanding record is boldly recorded. Chicago has honored his memory by creating Evans Street, which later was changed to Eighteenth Street. The city council noted again, by perpetuating his name with Evans Avenue, located in the city at 732 East. Nicholas Iglehart, known more for his outstanding reputation as a Chicago real estate promoter, reorganized the company with George and David Cage, hotel owners of the Brighton House and Tremont House and others; Andrew Brown, meat packer whose establishment was located on State Street; and Oramel S. Hough, with his packing house adjoining Archer Road in Bridgeport. Back in 1850, Brown and Hough were partners, and won first prize for their beef at the London exposition in 1852, awarding then a contract to supply meat for the English navy during the Crimean War, and in the following year their association was dissolved.

Some interesting excerpts taken from the document incorporating the Brighton Hotel and Stock Yard Company, signed by Governor William H. Bissell, February 14, 1857 read; "Be it enacted by the people of the State of Illinois, represented in the General Assembly that, George W. Gage, Andrew

Brown, David Gage, O.S. Hough and Nicholas P. Iglehart, and their successors are hereby constituted and declared a body corporate and polite. The said company shall have power to erect or purchase a Hotel, with suitable weighing scales and fixtures, out-houses, stables, barns, cattle pens, pasture grounds (and enclose the same), and all necessary or convenient appendage for cattle, sheep, hog and horse market, at or in the immediate vicinity of the town of Brighton in Cook County, Illinois, the Capital Stock of said Company shall be fifty thousand dollars, which may be increased from time to time to any sum not exceeding the entire amount extended on said Hotel, including cost of the same and all the appurtenance, and value of lends or lots thereunto belonging divided into shares of one hundred dollars each."

The colorful livestock enterprise located on Archer Road existed during difficult times, as the simple rural frontier was making a chaotic change to an industrial state. In the same year that the company was re-organized, the day of small things had passed Capitalist had much to seek at the hands of the state government. They called special sessions of the assembly where railroad and other corporations charters were acquired by none too scrupulous means. They swamped the available government machinery, besieged by requests for railroads and special charters, much like the incorporation of the Brighton Hotel and Stock Yard Company, also a special act passed by the General Assembly.

New railroads appeared with magical speed and began to crisscross the state. The once heralded advantage of the Brighton stock yards, of not having locomotives to frighten the stock became outmoded overnight. The iron horse gained the confidence of both the livestock men and businessmen, which dispersed much of the trade to newer stock yards, and to such distant cities as St. Louis and Cincinnati. By 1861, three notable stock yards in Chicago were competing with the

Brighton enterprise. The first, old Bull's Head, opened in 1848, at the intersection of Madison, Ashland and Ogden Avenues. The Brighton stock yards came next, in 1853, and two years later the Sherman "yards" were opened near the shores of Lake Michigan, adjoining the Illinois Central Railroad. In 1859, the fourth yard was opened by the Pittsburg and Fort Wayne Railroad in the vicinity of 20th and Canal Streets. As the Brighton stock yard business declined, Hough and Brown withdrew from the company as the Civil War started in 1861.

In an attempt to reaffirm Brighton's position as a popular livestock center, "Long John" Wentworth, Nicholas Iglehart, George and David Gage, influenced the officials of the United States Agricultural Society to consider permanently holding annual State Fairs at Brighton. They had emphasized the compromising advantages of Brighton's location at the outskirts of the city, that would serve both city dweller and farmer. Excerpts taken from the Chicago Tribune of Wednesday, September 11, 1861 read; "John Wentworth said that he leased the grounds to George W. Gage for Fairs, State, National and County, and for no other purpose. The war and the hard times had combined to depress Mr. Gage in his laudable efforts." The Tribune of Sunday, September 15th read; "Giving credit where credit is due, the highest need of praise must be given to William Derby for the design and erection of the best class of structure we have ever seen at a State Fair. These are intended to be permanent, and it is understood that some of our citizens are interested in an enterprise looking for annual Fairs at Brighton for a term of years,"

The early ownership of the Chicago Democrat newspaper by Long John Wentworth, had long alienated the competitive Chicago Tribune, who took every opportunity to challenge his motives. The early commentary in the Tribune about the State Fair at Brighton on Archer Road, was filled with flowery praise, but when inclement weather ruined the program, their editorial guns lambasted the disgraceful Brighton site selection. The Saturday edition of the Tribune of September 7th, before the fair commenced, read; "The State Fair Grounds at Brighton presented a busy scene at the time of our visit yesterday. Already numbers of horses and cattle are comfortably stalled, and others to arrive today, and rapidly from this time until the opening of the Fair. Whether "distance lends enchantment" to the State Fair in every respect as regards our citizens, the location is universally accepted as a happy compromise between city and country, just without the limits of the one, and with boundless continuity of prairie on the other. The State Fair is to open on the 9th inst. Monday, and continue open one week. It will bring thousands to our city, as an occasion on which the Railroads have all agreed to carry passengers at half fare. Such an opportunity for shopping and bargain hunting will not soon again occur for our country friends, and though this is war time, they are indispensable in the family and on the farm, not to be spared, and this will combine profit with pleasure in the coming Fair Week. The number of workmen has been enlarged, and the work goes briskly on. More than any of its predecessors, this Fair will be characterized by the feature of a mart, like the great Fairs of Europe."

"Thousands of dollars will change hands for fine stock, and buyers and sellers will be brought together in a noble display of cattle, horses, sheep and swine. How to reach the Fair from the city, it will be the care of the railroad men to demonstrate. Many will doubtless come in by their own teams. From the city to Brighton the routes offered are varied to suit every taste. The tugs on the river will land passengers at Bridgeport, one mile distant. This route does not promise much, but may after all be well patronized. Certainly, the tugs will run if business offers. The railroad tracks of the St. Louis, Alton & Chicago Railroad will be the main artery of communication, and by means of a half hour, trains will carry all that may desire, landing them directly on the north entrance of the Fair Grounds. As to drives in private or public vehicles, there is an even more varied opportunity for selection, and no one needs to ride in a thronged and dusty street."

Chapter 24: The Disastrous Deluge

The optimism for the opening of the State Fair continued to appear in the Tribune. The Sunday, September 8th edition read; "Personal", "Governor Yates has signified to the State Agricultural Society his acceptance of their invitation to attend the State Fair next week at Brighton." Another article in the same edition read; "To Exhibitors", "The entry books of the State Fair have been removed to the Fair Grounds at Brighton. They will remain open until Wednesday." A lengthier article the same day read; "The State Fair at Brighton", "From personal indications it is certain that the forthcoming Fair will be far more successful in every respect then the most sanguine friends of the project have dared to predict. Adamant Men interested in the various departments, are already arriving from distant portions of the country. Upwards of 1,0000 entries have been made, many of them from other States, and quite a number from New York, Connecticut, Massachusetts, and Canada. The Chicago & St. Louis Railroad have notified all other roads that our loads of stock that may arrive for the Fair need not be re-shipped; that they will ship the cars upon their roads and take them to and from the Fair Grounds without charge. The display of machinery promises to be very large. P.W. Gates & Company have erected a stationary engine upon the grounds for furnishing power for the exhibition of all the machinery engine upon the grounds for furnishing power for the exhibition of all the machinery requiring it. Fire-arms have already been entered from Massachusetts, Connecticut, Ohio and Illinois. Cheeny Bros. of South Manchester, Connecticut, are in the city, and have entered breech-loading rifles for infantry. The test for fire-arms will be a prominent feature. Heavily laden trains of articles for exhibitions are arriving upon every railroad. Fifteen car loads are now on the tracks of the Chicago Milwaukee Railroad. Nearly all the freight cars up on the Chicago & St. Louis Railroad, are engaged in advance until Tuesday noon. The same is true to some extent of all the railroads entering the city. As an additional attraction, Prof. C.W. Russell has made arrangements to send up balloons (12x25 feet) daily, during the Fair, free of charge. Two telegraph offices will be established on the rounds, one by the Company, the other in the railroad depot.

The Fair opened under ominous skies, an omen of the wretched weather that prevailed during the week of the event. Even the daily Tribune came under the weather as their narratives changed from earlier praise to bitter criticism. A summary of the week's reporting by the Tribune reads; Tuesday September 10th; "Opening Day of Exhibitions", "There was a dubious look in the sky early in the morning, and a little rain that discouraged many from attending. Wednesday, September 11th: "It rained, and rained steadily for most of the day. Of course nothing was done at the Fair. Thursday, September 12th; "Still Waiting for the Weather", "The clouds still supreme, and no blue sky to be seen to make a Dutchman a pair of trousers. Of course there was mud all around in the city and country, and no lack thereof at Brighten. As it was, there were six or seven thousand visitors, and the gate money reached $1500.00" On Friday, September 13th, the Tribune reads "25,000 People On The Grounds", "Yesterday dawned fair and cloudless, and held beautifully, clear throughout, the amphitheatre yesterday was well filled, and the work of the committee on Stock began." Another article in the same edition, of a humorous nature, read; "The Police Court At The State Fair", "Owing to the efficiency of the police at the Fair Grounds, and the significant legend near the main entrance, "Police Court", a large degree of order had been preserved, and evil doers have been content to confirm their rasealities to other points then the Fair Grounds. The only business of importance which had been transacted was the arrest of an indefinite number of unlicensed hucksters, peddlers, and other vendors, male and female, of pills, pies, peaches, and nostrums at stands outside the gate. The practices being in violation of the law, the parties were sentenced to pay the prescribed fines."

The hopeful view that Thursday's fair weather would prevail for the reminder of the weak was crushed the following day, as narrated in the Saturday, September 14th edition of the Tribune. "The State Fair At Brighton", "Yesterday was a beautiful and clear day, and a huge attendance south the Fair Grounds at Brighton. But the weather toward evening of yesterday assumed a lowering look, which boded ill for today, and at the present writing, the rain is falling fast, moves the pity for the Fair at Brighton." The Tribune's Sunday, September 15th edition summarized the ill-fated Fair; "Saturday saw the misfortune of the State Fair at Brighton culminate. The heavy rains of Friday night was too much for the susceptible soil of the locality, and the "power of mud" came out in full strength. We thought our experience as a resident of Chicago had fortified us against unpleasant novelties in the way of mud, but it seemed a deeper depth was reserved for Brighton. It is understood that some of our citizens are interested in an enterprise looking at annual Faire at Brighton for a term of years, now a failure as an investment. Never had Fair seekers suffered more discomforts. Those who want to Brighten by the roads, did do though unfragrant localities, for we do ever that Bridgeport is no garden of roses, and the slaughter houses and glue factories, in the vicinity, are to the nostrils unpleasant. The receipts for gate money on Saturday were only a few hundred dollars, and the appointment weak at the Fair was dismally ended."

With the failure of the State Fair on Archer Road, the proprietors of the Brighton livestock enterprise, never fully recovered, only to be dealt another blow when the new centrally located Union Stock Yards opened in 1865. The local "yards" passed into oblivion, although the Tribune of September 26, 1975, revealed that the facilities of early pens in Brighton still existed. "The distiller at this place though not working to its fullest capacity, is running favorably. From sixteen to twenty barrels of high wines are manufactured each day and about 400 head of cattle are fed in the shed adjoining." The beautiful Brighton race track and nostalgic Brighton House, fronting on Archer Road, continued to operate for a few years after the Civil War, as the site for city holiday picnickers. The following advertisement appeared in the Chicago Times, Monday July 2nd, 1866, with reference to a proposed Fourth of July programs at Brighton, "Special time table for July 4th; The Chicago & St. Louis R.H. will run a train to the Brighton Course as follows; Leave depot at 8:30, 9:55, 11:15 a.m., 12:35, 1:55, 3:15, 4:35, 5:55 P.M. Leave Brighton House at 9:15, 10:35, 11:35 a.m., 1:115, 2:35, 5:15, 6:35, and later if necessary. The Chicago & Great Eastern R.R. will run a train to the Brighton course. Fare 25 (cents) for a round trip, provided tickets are bought before entering the cars, otherwise double fares will be collected. Among the exercises will be national airs by the light guard band, reading the Declaration of Independence, an oration by Hon. J. L. Campbell of Iowa, singing of the "Red, White and Blue", and other songs by 100 young ladies, dancing on the green, foot races, sack races, female equestrianism, and other interesting games and sports."

The successful holiday affair at Brighton was summarized in the Chicago Times of Friday, July 6th, 1966, which read: "To all people the Fourth of July in our great city has become an intolerable nuisance and these are to be pitied who are not able to take the wings of the morning and fly away to the country where the sweet sounds of nature may be heard instead of those which emanate from gun powder. A very large number of citizens went out to Brighton where a varied and attractive programme had been prepared. Trains for the accommodation of Excursionists ran between the grounds and the city all day. The exercises were of an interesting character. One of the features of greatest interest was the drill of the Ellsworth Zouaves."

This outstanding organization was attributed to the late Elnor Ellsworth, the first officer killed in the Civil War. Impressed by the valor of the French Zouaves in the Crimean War, infantry men recruited from the Algerian tribe of Zouaves, Ellisworth, had organized his own company of cadets in Chicago, modeling the uniforms after those of the French troops. He was fanatic about discipline. The quality for membership in his corps, the cadets were required to sign a pledge of monastic severity. A cadet could be expelled from the group for "entering a drinking saloon at any hour, day or night." The cadets were famous for their precision drill. In 1860, challenging any similar organization to match their skill, they made a tour of the East for a series of contests. After appearances at West Point, New York, and other eastern cities, the Chicago Zouaves returned undefeated, marching from the railroad station with their uniforms adorned with ladies gloves, lace handkerchief's and dried and faded flowers. In his early death as the Civil War began, Ellsworth became an immediate personification of the Union war aims. "Remember Ellsworth" was the battle cry of the early months of the war, just as "Remember the Maine" and "Remember Pearl Harbor" served in later wars. Ellsworth was born in upstate New York in 1837. Of poor parents, he was truly a self made man. He hawked newspapers on trains, taught himself laboriously, read law while nearly starving as a copyist in a Chicago office. Fascinated by the military, he learned the complicated movements of the Zouave drill. Through his leadership of the cadets, he came to the attention of Abraham Lincoln, read law in Lincoln's office, participated in the campaign of 1860, commanded Lincoln's guards on the pre-inauguration trip to Washington, and became an intimate of the President's household. Ellsworth was a real charmer, good looking, smart, immensely personable, and a natural leader of men. He was killed by James W. Jackson, a hotel owner in Alexandria, Virginia, when Union troops removed a Confederate flag from the roof of the hotel. His drill team are reorganized as the Civil War ended, and shortly thereafter they made their appearance along Archer Road at the Brighton race track, July 4, 1866.

Chapter 26: Brighton's Conflagration

In February, 1867, the last of the early Chicago businesses finally abandoned the Brighton hotel and race track enterprise, selling their interests to its superintendent, John Lewis Baker, who paid $12,000 for the hostelery from Nicholas Iglehart and brothers, David and George Gage. Baker and his wife, Sarah, came from the East in 1861, when John came into the employ of the Brighton Enterprise as a veterinarian. When he came into possession of the Brighton House in 1867, he exerted every effort to restore its early reputation. Excerpts taken from a story in the Chicago Tribune read: "In February last, the property changed hands, Mr. Baker, the former superintendent becoming the owner, having purchased the entire property for a moderate sum of $12,000. Since the purchase, Mr. Barker has made extensive improvements costing not less than $5,000. Mr. Barker has given the "Brighton" a front rank among our suburban hotels."

Then nine months later, on Sunday, November 10, 1867, the front page of the Chicago Times was emblazoned with the following captions; "Disastrous Conflagration", "Total Destruction of Brighton House Property", "A Large Number of Animals Consumed", "Origin of the Fire", "Total Losses About $25,000". The narrative read: "A very disastrous fire occurred yesterday afternoon in the suburb of Brighton, which resulted in the complete demolition of the old landmark there, the Brighton House, together with the stables, sheds and appendage of that well known and well established hotel. The news of the configuration was received in town before dark last evening. The house, which was a very extensive wooden structure, which was built in 1854, and for a number of years had been owned and controlled by Messrs Gage of the Tremont House, under the supervision of Mr. John L. Baker."

"The house fronted upon the Archer road, the stables being several rods in the rear; to the southward, but connected with the house by the recently constructed sheds. To the westward of the stables was situated a large hay stack in which the first fire originated. The Great Eastern railroad tracks run diagonally past the site of the hotel, and a careful inquiry leaves no doubt that the fire had its origin from a locomotive, employed on this road. At about 3 o'clock in the afternoon, freight engine 29, belonging to the road, was standing attached to a freight train, directly opposite to the premises, upon a side truck, waiting for a train to pass. The locomotive was a wood burner and as it threw a volume of sparks and stood in that position for several minutes, it is supposed that the hay stack must have been ignited from the source. The hay stack stood near the barn, and with a strong wind blowing from the southwest, directly in that direction, it was but the work of a few moments and the whole was a seething cauldron of fire."

"From this point, the fire ran along the sheds, and in a very short time had communicated with the main building, and soon the whole was past human power to save. So rapid was the conflagration, and at the time of the day, so little assistance was available, that but very little could e removed. One or two of the city steamers located near the city limits hastened to the rescue, but were powerless to assist from the lack of any adequate supply of water. In a short time, the immense building was essentially in ruins, though the fire continued to carnival among the debris until a late hour last night. The McCaffery house (John McCaffery, "the father of Brighton") situated directly across the road, occupied as a hotel and grocery store, narrowly escaped destruction. The wind drove the flames very nearly in that direction and the board fence leading to the house ignited by the intense heat, and only by the most strenuous exertion was the latter house saved. It was impossible to make any close estimate of the loss last evening. The barn contained twelve valuable horses, eight head of young beeves, two buggies, and eighty tons of hay. Of these, only two horses are known to have got out, the remaining ten and the cattle being roasted alive, and their pitiful moans added not a little to the indescribable horrors of the scene."

"Mr. Baker paid Messrs. Gage, at the time of the purchase, $4,000, with this, the new furniture he had purchased and the stock that had been consumed in the stable, he estimated from $20,000 to $25,000; upon this he had not a dollar of insurance. The mortgages, Messrs Gage had insured the building for $8,000, the policies being taken out in their name and without any reference to Mr. Baker. This is the most disastrous fire that has occurred in this vicinity in a long time. It falls with particular severity upon Mr. Baker, who had been connected with the hotel for five or six years. Mr. Baker was away at the time of the fire, having gone to the cattle yards, intending to make some purchase of cattle. Before starting, he went to the trunk in his bedroom and taking out a roll of bills, containing $1500.00, he took $1000.00, about the amount he was intending to invest, and in a hurry of starting, instead of putting back the $500.00 in the truck, he placed it between the mattresses. The trunk was burned, both as if providentially, among the few articles saved, were the two mattresses, which had been carried out together, and, after the fire the roll of bills was found between them by an old lady, and returned to the owner intact."

Chapter 27: The Monster Balloon

The tragic destructions of the Brighton House property on Archer Road, coupled with other events in that year of 1867, created insurmountable obstacles for owner John Barker to overcome. Two new horse racing tracks were built within the city limits at the time, hurrying the end to the nostalgic Brighton trotting course. The Chicago Times dated Sunday, April 21, 1867 read; "Chicago Times dated Sunday, April 21, 1867 read; "Chicago needs a driving park. She is going to have two. The "Dexter" (nw. Cor. 47th & Halstead st.) will be recognized as the leading park in the northwest." Perseveringly, , tenacious John Baker went ahead, constructing a second Brighton House, and laid plans for the most spectacular Fourth of July program ever held on the adjoining race track.

The Chicago Times of Thursday, July 2, 1868, heralded the coming attraction by stating; "How Independence Day Can Be Enjoyed In Chicago." "At Brighton park the day will be observed on a grand scale. There will be a balloon ascension, a horse being attached to it, then there is to be a performance on a trapeze attached to the balloon. Dancing, sack races, wheel barrow and male races will constitute the other features of the occasion. The Archer avenue cars run to within a few blocks of the park, besides the St. Louis and Alton, and the Great Eastern railroads run near the park."

"The ascension of the monster balloon will commence as soon as the inflation is completed. The horse will be taken up at 4 pm. At 5 pm a trapeze performance by Mr. H. Lealie. Four well shaded dancing floors. Billy Nevins, American Cornet Band. The Archer road cars go to within 20 minutes walk to the gates. Mule race will come off over the one mile track." But faith was to administer the death blow to the remnants of the once colorful Brighton livestock enterprise, from which Mr. Baker never recovered. The tragic end was described in the Chicago Times of Sunday, July 5, 1868, which read: "The celebration at Brighton was a success in numbers and a failure in execution. During the day not less than 10,000 people visited the park. An excellent opportunity was offered the pleasure loving patriots to wander in an open field and enjoy the pure country air. No rude, uncouth, unsightly and disagreeable forest tree shut out the bright sunlight. Whole families, whole neighborhoods, the entire city in fact, were permitted to stroll the beautiful green award.

"But misfortune nevertheless elected Brighton park for the chose victim yesterday. The magnet which drew together the vast concourse of Chicago that depopulated the avenues, that left the marble fronts of the city deserted, was the monster balloon, "Chicago", which did not go up. On the contrary, it persisted in lying flat upon the ground, in defiance of all efforts at inflation. Like old bald-headed Elijah, it refused to "go up" for the edification of the little boys who surround it. The reason for the failure was twofold. In the first place, the teamster who carted the "monster" about the streets on Friday because inflated, or elevated, and failed to produce the great attraction upon the grounds until a very late hour at night, consequently, it is impossible to experiment with the "monster" until yesterday morning. When the experiment did take place, it was found that the hose which was intended to conduct the gas to the balloon was not strong enough to stand the press and on the first attempt, snapped in twain, thus rendering abortive all further efforts to send up the monster balloon "Chicago". Mr. J. L. Baker of the Brighton House, which is now being rebuilt, entertained the members of the press, with the substantials and delicacies of the sensor, and was set down by the Bohemians, as a man who "knows how to keep a hotel." The disappointing program culminated Baker's interest in the beautifully landscaped Brighton race track.

Thus the colorful enterprise on "Long John's" property since 1855, passed into oblivion thirteen years later. Wentworth started to lease the land by 1870 to truck farmers, two of which were Dan Ackerman and C.F. Claussen, who converted the race course into a dense cabbage patch for the manufacture of sauerkraut. "Long John's" death came in 1888, and not until 1901 was the west half of the property sold to the South Park Board for $85,827.50, by his nephew, Moses Wentworth. The remaining forty acres were purchased from the Wentworth family in 1906, expanding existing McKinley Park eastward to its present boundary.

Chapter 28: The Powder Hill Explosion

As the colorful Brighton livestock are on Archer Road ended, the second Brighton house became a symbolic landmark, representing the new period of manufacture and railroading in the nostalgic "town". With the termination of the Civil War in 1865, the expanded explosive industry sought new markets. Many were attracted to the Chicagoland area, where numerous quarries were being dug for clay to make bricks, and much dynamite was used for blasting. In 1866, noted Matthew Laflin established the first powder mill in Brighton, that later became the first St. Agnes church in the community. In 1888, the Oriental Powder Company purchased 16 ½ acres at Archer Road and Homan Avenue, and others soon followed. Excerpts found in an early community newspaper called the Vindicator, mentioned the industry in Brighton; "the whole neighborhood is occupied by powder magazines, there being no less than eight in a space covered by one block." Another edition stated; "all of the powder magazines in the vicinity of Chicago are located in and around Brighton. There are more than a dozen in the Town of Lake." The areas of unofficially titled "town of Brighton" is reality, lay in two other incorporated towns. The part of Brighton, south of Thirty-Ninth Street belonged to the Town of Lake, from 1865 until 1889. That portion of Brighton, north of Thirty-Ninth Street, was retained by the Town of Cicero from 1857 to 1889. Thus the great majority of Brighton's magazines at Archer Road and Homan Avenues were in the Town of Lake. The early community newspaper continued; "The magazines were substantially built of brick, two stories high with massive iron doors, and wish no more than one window, while most of them had skylights on the roof." Within a few years the following companies located in Brighton; the

American Powder Company, Hazard, Laflin and Rand, Oriental, Austin, Aetna, Forsyth and DuPont. When horse-drawn street carts from Chicago reached the town of Brighton over Archer Road in 1884, the explosive industry appeared in newspaper print with such excerpts; "the trucks were a new innovation and the powder wagons find the car tracks very useful. The teamsters wheel their vehicles upon them and avoid being stuck." Their callousness to danger was recalled in the memoirs of the late John J. McKenna, who was characterized as Mr. Hennessey in author Dunne's "Dooley Stories." "In the town of Brighton these powder houses were loaded with powder and dynamite, shipped it on cart s and wagons, sold it to quarries and various places where it was needed. The drivers were as careless in handling the dangerous explosives as if it had been limestone." Twenty years after the first powder magazine was erected along Archer Road, nature, not man's carelessness, was to cause an explosion of great magnitude.

The residents of Brighton, who had lived on a powder keg, dating back to 1866, were shocked into that reality the Sunday of August 29, 1886. The morning was overcast as the rain came pouring down, and flashes of lightening streaked through the sky when all at once the populace was startled by a tremendous explosion that shook their homes, shattered windows and overturned furniture. The following day the Chicago Daily News of Monday, August 30, 1886, was emblazoned with these captions; "Death From the Clouds", "Two Lives Lost And Many People Injured By The Explosion Of A Powder Magazine", "Wrecked Houses", "Blasted Trees and Rock Strewn Fields", "Immense Crowds Viewing Scene." The newspaper narrative read; "The casualties caused by the powder house magazine explosion which occurred yesterday morning are full and numerous and fatal, as at first reported. So far the fatalities amount to two and before night two other persons will in all probability die. Dead; Carrie B. Earnsworth 14 years old; George Kann, 35 years old. Fatally injured; John Guhl, 40 years old, driver for the Laflin and Hand Powder Company; Mrs. John Guhl, his wife, 24 years old; Mrs. Eliza Devine, 63 year old widow, Jason Shannon, 16 years old; Seriously hurt; William Kelly, 14 years old; Daniel Kelly, 14 years old, brother of the former; John Madden, a small boy; Phillip Bowler, arm crushed by flying stones and amputated; John Lorden Jr, 17 years old, leg badly crushed; Lesser casualties; John Jung, 52 years old, gardener, living south of Archer avenue; Mrs. Jung, 46 years old, wife of the former; Peter Hamm, 26 years old, gardener; Miss Kenny, 18 years old, parents reside on Johnson street, a quarter of a mile from the scene."

"At 9:30 am. Yesterday morning the residents of the city were startled by what seemed to be a tremendous clash of thunder. Buildings trembled and shook, windows were shattered and furniture overturned. The shock felt so severely all over the city was caused by the explosion of the magazine of the Laflin and Rand Company, when struck by a flash of lightning during a storm. There was a vivid flash of the electrical fluid, when a shaking of the ground, instantly followed by a dull red glare and a roar that was heard for miles around. People rushed from their homes and saw a monstrous black cloud hovering over Brighton Park. Afraid to approach the scene, they stayed around their homes until the fire engines dashed up and then the awe-stricken populace went to work like heroes, searching among the ruins of the surrounding houses for the dead and wounded. Hardly forty feet from the funnel-shaped hole, which marked the spot on which the magazine stood, was the ruin of the house of John Cuhl, the store-keeper and driver of the powder company. A few feet from the ruins, just across the ditch in the rear of the house, lay the body of pool little Carrie Farnsworth, who lived with the

Cuhls. She at the time of the explosion had been standing at the kitchen door and had been thrown by the shock several feet distant. Her curly yellow hair was a mass of blood, while her left side was ripped open and her left arm was torn from its socket. The blue eyes were half closed and the mouth bore a peaceful expression which showed that the violent death had been a painless one. The body was tenderly carried to a quieter spot."

"Working like beavers, the neighbors tore through the debris of the house and uncovered the body of John Cuhl, its owner, who had been outdoors with his wife when the explosion occurred, and who had been struck and covered by the ruins of the house. He was severely injured around the head and arms, his face was fearfully burned, his collar bone, leg and three ribs were broken, and he was seriously injured internally. He was unconscious. There is no chance for her recovery. Just across the street, Mrs. Devine's little house was now a heap of ruins, and its owner lay groaning with pain, with a heavy rafter across her limbs, both of which were broken. Mrs. Devine was past middle age and scarcely survived the terrible shock. She was taken to the county hospital in a patrol wagon. A short distance down the road and directly opposite the site of the Laflin and Rand exploded magazine, the searchers found the remains of a team of horses attached to a farmers wagon. The head of one of the horse was torn off and the other was frightfully mangled. Across the ditch lay the body of the driver and owner of the team, George Kann, a young farmer living at Auburn Station, Illinois. He was totally unconscious and brutally bruised by the flying bricks and timber. He was taken to the county hospital, where he died."

"Justice Tearney's house in the Town of Lake, lived a short distance from the scene (4600 Archer Road). He was asleep and was awakened by the noise to see the surrounding country through what had been the front of the house. The east side and front had been blown away and the justice's little boy, Gilbert, was severely injured by the flying fragments. A man named Phillip Bowler, who was in a wagon with Joe Devroe, was struck with a brick which broke his right arm. Pater Hamm, who was also with them, was severely cut in the face and was taken to the county hospital. Not far from the exploded house was the powder house of the Hazard Powder Company. Strange as it seems, this was the only other house damaged by the explosion containing powder and dynamite. A huge hole 25 feet deep, 60 feet wide and 100 feet in length, marks the spot occupied by the exploded magazine. For fifty feet around the ground is clear of everything, and even the hole is free of debris."

"Besides the wreck of the Hazard Company's magazine, the explosion caused more or less damage to the other powder houses in the vicinity, but failed to explode any of the dynamite and powder, which they contained. In the Hazard magazine there were 70,000 pounds of powder, and from 1000 to 3000 sticks of dynamite. In the Austin magazine was 60,000 pounds of powder, in the Oriental 1000 pounds, and in the Aetna and Forsyth magazine were 50,000 pounds of powder each. The barn of the Oriental Powder Company was totally demolished and the horses killed. The ruins caught fire, but the flames were extinguished before they could spread to the magazine. The force of the explosion was demonstrated in various ways. One of the strongest was the tearing up of the potato field in the vicinity. The entire crop lay on the surface of the ground and was all ready to be collected and sent to market. A stone weighing fully one hundred pounds was thrown across the field, striking and cutting a small tree on the opposite side. With undiminished force it leveled a cabbage field, tearing up the vegetables, and leaving a black furrow in its wake for several hundred feet."

"John Kelly was walking along a road a quarter of a mile from the scene, and was thrown some distance through the air and alighted in a haystack, insensible, but unhurt. Hoh Jung, a Hollander, loving opposite Justice Tearney, was sitting at the window when the glass crushed at his feet. His wife and the children were hurled to the floor. A moment later he heard two more explosions in succession, which shook his house from top to bottom. Two stones which were a part of the exploded magazine were hurled through the roof and came to rest in his attic. Charles Vahmeyer, a clerk from the Laflin and Rand Company, lived about a quarter of a mile from the scene and when the storm of flying stones and timber filled the air, he took his family to his barn for protection. A stone which crashed through the house window grazed the head of Mary Farnsworth, the sister of the dead Carrie. The Laflin and Rand Powder Company estimate their losses at $15,000 to $20,000."

Chapter 29: Inquisitive Visitors

At the time of the explosion, William Smith, a compositor for the Chicago Daily News was visiting his brother-in-law on Archer Road in Brighton. He wrote the following article for his newspaper; "The flash of the explosion seemed to fill the air. It was like sheet lightning, except that it was red. For half an hour the excitement at Brighton Park was intense. Every house was damaged as if by an earthquake and nobody knew what caused it. The people ran about wildly, the women screamed and the scene was indescribable, until the report came that the powder magazine had blown up."

"All Bridgeport accepted the event as intended for the especial pleasure, and crows poured afoot, and by shaky and odd looking vehicles until Archer Avenue was black with the swarms. Fully 5,000 people must have visited the scene by noon. They were not dismayed by the mile and a half stretched of muddy road that lies between Western avenue, terminal point of the street cars, and the group of magazines at Archer and Homan avenue. There were a good many saloons along the road, provided for the accommodation of thirsty farmers and brick yard employees. Many of their large front windows were broken by the explosion. The inquisitive visitors stopped in to quench their thirst and hear the story of how the window was broken. One of the beer dispensers, whose window had not been broken, did not intend to allow valuable customers to slip away for the lack of an attraction. He rolled an immense boulder from back yard and placed it near his front door, where everybody who passed could see it. Although he was located three quarters of a mile from the scene, his supply of beer soon ran out."

Brighton's resident, John J. McKenna, who author Finley Peter Dunne characterized in his "Mr. Dooley Stories", also contributed his experience of the munitions explosion. "I lived near the corner of Archer Road No 1 Rockwell Street, where the street car barns are now located. It was then a large grove. I remember our house being split open along the top of the roof and the rain came pouring in knocking all the plaster off the wall. All the houses that were within six miles of the powder house had the windows broken; lamps fell off the mantel piece and pictures dropped from the walls. The many people who attended St Agnes church were fortunate to have left church just about fifteen minutes before the explosion, which blew all of the windows out of the church. The concussion was so strong that it knocked the windows out of a building located on the northeast corner of Wabash avenue and Monroe street. All the windows of the Chicago and Alton round house (37th and California avenue) were shattered, and in all the buildings that were two stories high, facing west for four miles around. The explosion created such a sensation that for at least three weeks people came from all parts of the city to visit the scene. On the day after the explosion, a mass meeting was held, and although I had attended many meetings I have never seen one where it was so easy to obtain the enthusiastic cooperation of the people. Everyone was very indignant and agreed that the powder houses must go. They all had to move out and bought land near Blue Island. Within a short time there were no powder wagons or powder houses anywhere near the village of Brighton or along Archer Road."

Chapter 30: "Archey Road's" Mr. McKenna

When the noted author Finley Pater Dunne's "Mr. Dooley" sketches became popular during the Chicago World's Fair in 1893, he took John J. McKenna of "Archey Road" from real life as his characterization of "Mr. Hennessey". John J. was born in Grassy Point, New York, on the west bank of the Hudson River in 1857. His father, William, was a skilled brick burner by profession and migrated to Chicago in the same year his son was born. They made their first home at 18th Street and the Chicago River, and from there started to move southwestward, as old clay holes were abandoned and new ones were started,. In 1866, the McKenna's lived in Bridgeport at 35th Street, on the banks of the South Fork of the Chicago River. Six years later the United States Brick Company erected a large plant in Brighton at Kedzie Avenue and the Illinois and Michigan canal. The new enterprise attracted the McKenna's, who made their new home on the brick yard's property. In the following year of 1873 the new company went bankrupt during a most serious depression; the McKenna's abandoning the site for a new home in the vicinity of 22nd and Blue Island Avenue.

In 1874, father William McKenna was able to acquire the clay hold site from the O.L. Mann Brick Company that was located in Brighton on California Avenue, adjoining Archer Road, that has since become the location of the Chicago Park District's, Kelly Park. He developed a thriving brick manufacturing business, which permitted him to put his son John through Bryant and Stratton Business College, and soon after became an associate in his father's business. It was not until 1881 that the McKenna's returned to make residence in Brighton. Their new home was located at the corner of Archer Road and Rockwell Street, surrounded by a beautiful grove that became known as McKenna's Woods. Many years later the site was cleared for the construction of a street car barn in 1908, which presently serves as the Chicago Transit Authority's bus depot.

John J. McKenna entered politics, being elected town of Cicero assessor in 1883, and from 1885 to 1889, he served as president of the board. Before Brighton's memorable munitions explosion in 1886, the American Powder Company, located near the McKenna's residence, abandoned one of its buildings on Archer Road to the Brighton government. The following article making reference to Mr. McKenna and the abandoned powder house, appeared in the early community Vindicator newspaper dated Saturday, October 25, 1885. It read; "The finishing touches are now being put on the Brighton Town Hall, alias, Old Powder House. Invitations are out for a grand ball given by the citizens of Brighton Park on Tuesday evening next in the time honored edifice. Mr. McKenna has been instrumental in procuring appropriations of several hundred dollars from the Cicero Town Board. Hence the celebration."

William McKenna retired from the family brick company in 1887, where after son John developed the enterprise into a thriving business, producing 75,000 bricks per day, and conducting his business from offices located at 177 LaSalle Street. When Chicago celebrated the Columbian World's Fair in 1893, the country was under the strain of a serious depression, during which time John McKenna had mortgaged his business to purchase new pumps, resulting in his bankruptcy, losing everything after an investment of approximately $70,000. In 1896, he served as a member of the State Board of Equalization that lasted for six years. After a period of short terms as a member of various state and county committees, he accepted an appointment as Chief Inspector of Private Employment Agencies in 1917, and retained that position until his retirement in 1938. Thereafter, he turned to writing reminiscent poems and memoirs of early Chicago and Brighton, and became popularly known as the "poet of Archey Road." He wrote two books, "The Reminiscence of the Great Chicago Fire of 1871", and Sun Worshippers of McKinley Park." Colorful John J. McKenna died February 18, 1941, at the age of eighty-four. In his lifetime he had seen Archer Road transformed from a stock yard trail into a thriving metropolitan thoroughfare, over which distant international travelers come, traversing between downtown Chicago and the popular Midway airport.

Chapter 31: Summit

As Archer Road leaves the boundaries of the city of Chicago, it passes over an imperceptible crest in the adjoining village of Summit, recognized as one of the most unique continental divides in our nation. It is a ridge, which although low and inconspicuous, separates two vast watersheds. On the one side, the surplus rain and snow waters naturally drain toward Lake Michigan. This surplus, combined with that from the watersheds of the other Great Lakes, eventually flow into the St Lawrence River, which empties into the Atlantic Ocean. On the other side of the divide, water drains toward the Desplaines and Kankakee Rivers, and thence down the Illinois River to the Mississippi, which empties into the Gulf of Mexico. The lowness of the divide as Summit facilitated the early construction of railroads and highways with a minimum of difficulty. Southwest, near the village of Summit, it is only fifteen feet above the surface of Lake Michigan, and this is known as the Chicago Outlet, one of the greatest natural passes in America, and the gateway to the Illinois Valley. At one time, thru this Outlet during extreme floods, the Desplaines River uniquely overflowed, sending its excessive waters eastward over the divide, thru Mud Lake, and thence into the South Branch of the Chicago River. This was the route of the famous Chicago Portage, traveled by early explorers, missionaries and traders. It facilitated the building of the Illinois and Michigan canal in 1836, and its by-product, the adjoining Archer Road passing through the heart of Summit. Of its early history, Andreas the noted historian wrote; "The first house built in Summit was the stage ranche on the location of the hotel now (1884) kept by Dennis O'Brian, erected by Russell K.

Heacock about 1836. Other narrators state that the ranch was built by the stage company about 1835, and that it was subsequently bought by Heacock." The life of this colorful personality describing his intimate association with the history of Archer Road is narrated in greater detail under the title "Stage Coaches Over Archer Road."

Earliest Summit served as an important "Y" junction, with the stem connecting that point with Chicago. Over the southwest branch came farmers wagons and livestock drives from such settlements as Hickory Creek and Palos. The other branch of the "Y" crossed the Desplaines River at Summit, connecting the popular trail along the north side of the waterway to Joliet and points far beyond. Russell Heacock is credited with building the first bridge over the river in Summit, attracting business to his stage ranche located on Archer Road and Harlem Avenue. This route became a very important wagon trail, as revealed in the manuscript left by an early settler, A Van Dyke Pierson, which he called the "Chicago Trail". After his death, the family had his narrative published in the Illinois Historical Society Journal in 1918. Excerpts taken from that article read; "The story of the highway from Bloomington to Chicago started in 1831. The Desplaines was crossed at Van Huston's. The road ran along the west side of the Desplaines, forty or fifty miles, crossing over the east side at Summit, continuing on the east side, passing through Brighton, and entered Chicago at Archer Avenue, then known as Archer Road, Chicago at that time had a population of about 150. There were no roads, nothing by prairie, with an occasional Indian trail, until they came to Joliet. Here the trails became more marked, and the indication of the white man's presence became more evident. With the coming of the railroad, this old wagon road, like Othello, found its occupation gone, although cattle continued to be driven on it from Lexington to Chicago, until along in the sixties. This old road grew out of the country's road, and was a mighty factor in developing our country, as well as the great city by the lake." The route described by Mr. Pierson was also the initial stage coach road to Joliet, Ottawa, Peru and Peoria, until the Archer trail was improved as the "canal road" in 1836. Thereafter the omnibuses followed the full length of Archer Road to Joliet before crossing the Desplaines River to reach Ottawa and the other towns beyond. Mr. Pierson never realized that one day the old Chicago Trail would be succeeded by the nationally prominent Route 66, leading to his nostalgic Lexington and Bloomington, as well as Springfield and St. Louis.

Chapter 32: Long John Wentworth

The colorful history of the early Archer Road is deeply entwined with the innumerable activities of gruff, argumentative, Long John Wentworth. The deep chested, three hundred pound individual, standing six foot, six inches tall, was to overshadow Russell K. Heacock's early prominence in the history of distant Summit and Archer Road. The Wentworth family first came to America in 1735, and two later descendants became governors of the State of New Hampshire. While Governor Wentworth labored in 1770 to hold his colony loyal to the King of England, a distant cousin, Colonel John Wentworth presided in the 1774 revolutionary convention in New Hampshire. His son John Jar represented the state in the Continental Congress and signed the Articles of Confederation. His great-grandson, Long John Wentworth was born March 5, 1815, in Sandwich, New Hampshire. He was to follow the course of empire to Chicago, and make the name Wentworth as famous upon the prairies, as it had been in upper New England.

He taught school for one winter before entering Dartmouth College in 1832. Upon graduation in 1836, he went to Michigan seeking employment as a teacher. When he could not find work in Detroit, he walked to Ann Arbor and Ypsilanti, and then back to Detroit. From there Wentworth sent his trunk to Chicago by the brig "Manhattan" and took the stage to Michigan City. From there he walked the lake beach to Chicago, arriving with $30.00. He ate his first meat at the boarding house of Mrs. Harriet Austin Murphy at Lake and Wells streets, October 25, 1836. Thereafter, for the next forty-nine years he celebrated the advent of having dinner with Mrs. Murphy if he was in the city at the time.

Within a month after his arrival he became editor of the Chicago Democratic newspaper. Three years later, he became its owner, after paying $2,800 for the business. In 1840 he made it Chicago's first daily newspaper. Wentworth returned East in the following year to attend Harvard, and passed the bar shortly thereafter. In 1845, at the age of twenty-eight, he served in the House of Representatives, as the youngest member of its body. In the twenty-five years that he owned the Democratic newspaper he used it most effectively to elevate his colorful and controversial career. Long John served seven terms as a Congressman in Washington. When he campaigned for office, he was often seen out among the Illinois and Michigan canal workers, looking for votes. He always came in company with a man who carried a jar of whiskey, strapped to his back, from which he treated comforted voters.

By mid-century, with the canal completed and Archer Road improved, and the building of railroads accelerating, the Chicagoland area was ripe for another feverish real estate boom. Under such favorable conditions John Wentworth started laying the foundation for a large fortune by purchasing vast areas of land dating back to 1845 when land averaged about $20.00 an acre. Archer Road passed through two of his large holdings, one in Brighton, and the other at Summit, each with its own colorful history during the time he possessed them. Ever since the early 1850's, Wentworth's farm in Summit had been "the jewel of all his possession". The farmhouse, still standing off the northeast corner of Archer and Harlem Avenues, was built about 1858. It was large and comfortable, but designed for utility, rather than display. The surrounding expanse of acres, given no fancier name than "John Wentworth's Farm", became a model of efficiency, and a center of experimentation of agricultural methods. The farm was not Long John's home, but his retreat. He loved to take a party of friends aboard the Chicago and Alton cars for the ten mile trip to Summit, and a tour of inspection. There, in his private enclave of nearly seven square miles, where his despotic will was subject to no veto, he could shape the corner of the world completely to his liking. The size of the farm on Archer Road never satisfied Wentworth. His desire for land was insatiable. In 1854 he purchased the square mile bounded by Ashland Avenue, 31st Street, Western Avenue, and 39th Street, through which Archer Road passed diagonally, and where the colorful Brighton race track was to be built in the following year. In 1850 he bought an additional six hundred acres for his Summit farm, and by the eve of the Civil War, the farm had grown to 2,000 acres, one fifth of them improved. For the census of 1860, Long John estimated its cash value at $50,000, and listed a total of 60 horses, 30 milk cows, 2 oxen, 275 other cattle, 300 sheep.

For everyday living he preferred the hotel suite of the bustling city, where his noted accomplishments evolved. In 1857 he because mayor, serving one year without salary. Wentworth was the first to introduce the steam fire engine called "Long John", and in the same year created the initial paid fire department. In 1860 he was re-elected mayor, and some years later during the Civil War, Wentworth became the commissioner of police, frustrating a threatened raid aimed at releasing Confederate prisoners at Camp Douglas located at East 50th Street and South Cottage Grove Avenue. As a legislator, his final term in Congress extended from 1865 to 1867.

Chapter 33: Something of Everything

During the years of 1869 and 1876, Wentworth acquired more than a thousand additional acres in the neighborhood of Summit, at a cost of no less than $170,000. In the 1880's the estate included approximately three thousand acres of contiguous land, and another thousand acres of scattered plots lying south and east. To the census taker in 1880, Wentworth declared that he had 2,400 acres of tilled land and 2,100 acres of permanent meadows, pastures, orchards, and vineyards. He now valued the Summit farm at $460,000, or more than nine times its worth twenty years before. Big flocks of chickens, ducks, geese, and turkeys, in numerous varieties, were a part of Long John's plan to have "something of everything". A visitor in 1861, noted colonies of bees and admired an orchard of one thousand apples and pear trees on the sandy ridge, that out the farm from east to west. In the fields grew oats, wheat, corn, and potatoes, even some tobacco, for use in the battle against sheep ticks. Some products like wool, butter, poultry were marketed regularly, but most of the food produced was consumed right on the farm by the livestock, the pack of dogs, and the scores or more of farmhands, whom Wentworth employed on a year around basis.

Wentworth, was for many years the leading advocate and practitioner of livestock improvement in northern Illinois. His farm produced only little for the market. Its main purpose was the breeding of thoroughbred stock for sale to other farmers. The Summit herds were therefore never large, the pastures never crowded. The emphasis was always upon quality, rather that quantity. He bought his blooded animals from Eastern importers, and knew their ancestry almost as well as he knew his own. The English Durham, the Shorthorn, most important of all pure breeds in the grading up of American beef cattle, inevitably became a specialty on the Summit farm. But he preferred the Alderney, declaring that it would be his choice if he could keep but a single cow. To stock the farm with sheep, Wentworth at first chose both the French Merino, or Rambouillets, renowned for its fine wool. As for hogs, Wentworth was perhaps the country's most enthusiastic champion of the Suffolk breed, a variation upon the Small Yorkshire. The authority of Charles S. Plumb, even credits him with the first importation of Suffolk swine into the United States, although it is more likely that he started his herd with purchases from Eastern breeders. Suffolks was small in size, but inexpensively kept. He maintained in 1869, that by pasteurizing them for five months of the year, and feeding them corn during the other seven, he could produce pork of the very best quality, for two cents a pound. In the columns of the Prairie Farmer, over a forty year period, one finds frequent mention of Wentworth's livestock sales to purchasers, near and far. In October 1875, for example, the paper reported that he had recently sold ten Suffolk boars and five sows, seven Southern bucks and nine ewes, together with a Shorthorn bull, to a total of fourteen farmers scattered through Illinois, Iowa, Missouri, Wisconsin, Michigan, Ohio, and Pennsylvania. During his first decade of stock breeding, Wentworth's cattle, sheep and hogs won many premiums at the annual fairs. Many were probably won at the Illinois State Fair held on his property in Brighton, located on Archer Road in 1881, six miles northeast of his Summit farm. The site of the fair in that year was held on the Brighton race track, adjoining the early Brighton stock yards and drovers hotel. The property was retained by the Wentworth family from 1854 until 1906, eighteen years after Long John's death. Although his pursuits have been minutely recorded, his holdings and activities on the Brighton scene, retain an air of mystery, never correlated by historians or biographers.

Once Long John's reputation was firmly established as a livestock breeder, he showed less interest in grooming animals for exhibition, but he never ceased to encourage all efforts at closer cooperation among farmers, both for the exchange of information and for political purposes. At the time of his return to Congress in 1865, he was vice president of the Illinois State Agricultural Society, and a member of its executive committee. His participation in politics after 1872 became intermittent and erratic. Little remained of his old appetite for public office. He declined to run for state senator in 1874, and although nominated for alderman two years later, he retired from the contest before the election. On one occasion, it is said a group of citizens visited his farm house on Archer Road in Summit, to suggest that he become a candidate for mayor. Long John, whom they found sitting contently in the shade of an apple tree, gave them a terse reply; "Gentlemen, I'm happy here. Take an apple." In 1882, he confided to friends; "So many people visit my farm in the course of a year that it is very difficult to remember them."

The colorful life of John Wentworth came to an end October 16, 1888, at the age of seventy-three. He never did see the erection of the fifty ton monument that stood seventy-three feet high, estimated at a cost of $38,000, which he ordered himself. It stands conspicuously in Rosehill cemetery, symbolizing his stature in the annals of Chicago's early history. After his death the enormous farm was gradually dissolved, and with the passing of years, Summit became a thriving village, when the gargantuan Corn Products Company came to erect the world's largest corn refinery. It remains the main source of employment for the villagers, numbering 1700 persons, when working at capacity, grinding as much as 80,000 bushels of corn a day. Here corn is processed into syrup, starch, cooking oil, and scores of by-products used in the manufacture of candy, chewing tobacco, beer, mucilage, fireworks, ink and stationary. Unchanged from the days of old, its importance as a significant road junction, continues to pulsate the heart of Summit. The nostalgic village was once dissected by early trails that have since been transformed into thriving thoroughfares named Archer Road, Harlem Avenue, and Route 171. The latter crosses over the Desplaines River, where pioneer Russell K. Heacock built the first bridge, to connect with the trail that has become today's famed Route 66.

Chapter 34: St. James at the Sag Outlet

Long before the arrival of the first American settler, the hills and valleys of the beautiful Sag, through which Colonel Archer later succeeded in constructing his top grade road, had been active with Indian life and warfare, of French exploration, or missionary teaching, and of trade of which we still have evidences, and year by year are uncovering more. The ruins of the old fortification, which commanded an extensive view of the Sag Valley, became a French mission that is known today as St James at the Sag, located at the junction of 107th Street and Archer Road. Curious implements of war are continuously being turned up in the region, definitely pointing to ancient hostilities. The stone "squaws" hoes suggest Indian tilling of the soil. We see signs of chipping stations where the stone hatchets and arrow heads were made. All these and the countless trails, leading in all directions, predicate the steady thread of occasioned feet, going to show that these hills and forests, valleys and streams, formed a broad and fitting stage for the drama that was being performed by bronze skinned actors. Nature here supplied them with all their needs and provided material and media for their art and adornment. Fish and game for their meat, wild rice and their own primitively cultivated corn, with wild leaves and roots for vegetables. Abundant water flowed from the cool springs for their drink, and furs and hides provided their clothing. The wild flowers, hut hulls, roots and bark were their native dyes.

Then came the French explorers; Perot in 1671; Marquette and Joliet in 1673; LaSalle and Tonty in 1681, all familiar with the Sag Valley and its inhabitants traversing over the ancient Archer Indian trail. Following them were other missionaries and traders, and a new order prevailed. The good Fathers preached love and good will, penitence and forgiveness, from the established mission at the base of Sag hill, overlooking the junction of Stoney Creek and the Desplaines River. In the meantime the traders plied their business among their red brother, bargaining for rich furs in return for trinkets, blankets, and the like. They built early forts along the Archer trail. The French official, Durantaye, erected one at its east end, on the shores of Lake Michigan in 1685, another at the Sag Outlet, still another in today's Higginbotham's Woods at Hickory Creek. They left evidences of their visit, at the Sag and 107th Street, in section 18, Mr. Thomas Kelly in 1856, found a pair of metal soles, such as the French soldiers wore in olden times, and he discovered a skeleton of a man with an ancient French gun and powder horn of copper, with the inscription "FraryBinhem", etched upon it. Both French and Spanish coins have been found in hollow trees, and underground in different parts of the Sag Valley, indicating that more than one soldier of fortune had cached his treasure in the hills adjoining Archer Road.

In the Palos hills, a short distance to the south, the late Christopher Mikelson discovered many years ago, old French coins in a hollow tree, near the present ski jump in Swallow's Cliff Forest Preserves, while in more recent years, Mrs. Maude MahaffayTraub uncovered a number of very old French and Spanish coins in her father's grape arbor in Palos Park. The Sauganash trail, that became a segment of the Widow Brown's Road leading to Hickory Creek in 1831, and now known as LaGrange Road, was the site of an old Indian fort, just above the ford of the Sag canal. It was near this spot in what was later the Theodore Lucas farm, that two French axes were found some years ago. But the early French were explorers, missionaries, and traders, more than they were settlers, and the clash with the English for the fur trade was inevitable. The military decisions of the War of 1756-63 were to come in the fields remote from Archer Road passing through the Sag Valley, but which resulted in the Treaty of Paris in 1763. It ceded to England, all France had claimed east of the Mississippi River. So passed the French regime that ruled the Sag region.

Starting sometime around 1836, a small settlement developed at the Sag Outlet during the construction of the adjoining Illinois and Michigan canal, and its by-product, the improved Archer Road, passing through the Sag Valley to connect Chicago with Lockport. The Sag was a post office hamlet by 1838, boasting of a store and hotel, the latter kept by Joshua Bell. Chief engineer, James M. Bucklin, who laid out the course the canal was to follow, revealed the origin of the name Sag, as being derived from the local Indian name of Ausoganashkee, meaning "reed swamp". Some years later Stoney Creek was excavated to become the "Feeder" for the Illinois and Michigan canal, and acquired its own distinction as the Sag canal. The early frame St James church at the base of the hill that overlooked the junction of both canals, served the construction crew that built them. Many settled in the vicinity after completing their labors. In the church cemetery located on a breathtaking slope, can be found the names of many early settlers of the Sag. One can find the grave of Alexander Reid, merchant and postmaster of the Sag settlement until 1855. It is said that Raid was a partner of Marshall Field, in Field's first store, an old stone building still standing at the junction of 111th Street and Archer Road. Also to be found in the St James cemetery are the graves of Jacob and Halena Koller of Willow Springs, oldest living members of the parish at one time. Jacob had been president of Willow Springs, and highway commissioner for twenty-five years. The famous little red school house in the adjoining Palos Forest Preserves, now a nature museum, was built by his father, who had moved into the region in 1840.

Chapter 35: An Irish Burial

In 1852, a new St James church was built on the summit of the hill located at 107th and Archer Road, under the guidance of its pastor, Father Ballman, a true and watchful shepherd of his flock. His was a beautiful charity for the weak and reckless, but he knew when to be stern. There was the time that the party of mourners from the Chicago community of Bridgeport, took possession of the good Father's house. It had been stipulated in the deed to the eight acres comprising the church yard of St James, given in 1858 by Mr. and Mrs. James Murphy and Mr. and Mrs. John Sullivan, that all graves should be free. It soon followed that people from Brighton Park and Bridgeport, down Archer Road, came out to take advantage of this philanthropic provision. For that purpose one winter day, a funeral party from the two distant communities came out on the Alton to bury a body, arriving at eight o'clock in the morning. They buried the dead, but there was no train back until dark. It was a long cold wait, so, after several drinks in the settlement, they invaded Father Ballman's parish house. The priest was away, and only the housekeeper, who was baking bread, was at home. She ran screaming and locked herself in a cold room upstairs, where she almost froze. The crowd ate all the fresh bread, build a big fire in the stove, and were having a merry time when Father Ballman returned.

"I wonder who his Giblets is?" asked one fellow, not recognizing the priest who stood in the doorway, looking in astonishment at his rowdy visitors, occupying every available seat. "Say, Mister," the fellow continued hospitably, "if ye can find a place to sit down, then sit down sir." "I am very thankful to you for your hospitality", replied the priest, recovering himself, "but this is my house, and I as pastor of this parish", he added sternly. "And I want to see you fellows get out of here quickly. Now move!" And they did move, suddenly sobered and profuse in their apologies. That is, the men moved, but the priest told the women and children to remain indoors until train time. Father Ballman's strong hand and gentle spirit wrought much good among his people, lifting up and giving hope to those in trouble and steadying the weak and wavering in those turbulent days.

The Sag settlement had never grown large under the shadows of adjoining Lemont's prosperity, with its wealth of stone quarries. St James Church, standing high on the hill overlooking the Sag Outlet, remains as a reminder of the days gone by, nestled amid verdant forests or exquisite beauty, nature's antidote to a turbulent metropolis. Its charming lanes and winding roads search over hill and glen for the interesting varieties of man's estate. Down on the opposite of St James, scientists are tussling with the problems of atomic energy at the Argonne National Laboratory.

Many of the residents in the surrounding Sag Valley come to St James to worship, reminded by its architecture of their mother churches in Europe. The deep brown beams of Sitka Spruce from Alaska, constitutes its roof and arches. When the original frame church was abandoned at the base of the hill in 1852, the present one was constructed on the summit, overlooking the beauty of the Sag region. Engraved on the church window panes are the names of such early parishioners as; John Bremner and his family ancestors of the Bremner Biscuit & Company family. In the adjoining church cemetery on the slopes of the hill, are burials dating back to 1830, revealing many Irish, German and Dutch names, recalling those who helped dig the old Illinois and Michigan canal and the nostalgic Archer Road.

The original character and traditions of St James have been perpetuated by its able pastor, Reverend Raymond Plozynski, admired by all for his endowed razor sharp wit. The Father is a tall, husky, outdoor type of man, who had adopted a policy of preserving the old, while blending in the new. As a youthful student of the seminary, he worked during vacations saving lives, before his assignment of saving souls. He had worked for the former South Park Board during the summer months as a life guard to Jackson Park. Father Plozynski had attained quite a reputation along Archer Road in the vicinity of the Sag, breeding boxer dogs during his leisure. Spiritually, he perpetuated the tradition of three centuries, by performing the unchanged ritual of mass that the early French missionaries initiated at the Sag. His active congregation numbering some 125 families, are to be seen celebrating mass with him, held at 8:30 and 10:15 am on Sunday's, and 7:00 am on week days.

The township of Palos, embracing the beautiful Sag Valley, contributed to the early commercial importance of Archer Road, as it passed diagonally through the northwest corner of the district. Branching south from Archer Road, and dividing the Palos township in half, was the Sauganash Indian trail, that was integrated with the former road in 1851, as the new Cook County highway called the Widow Brown's Road. The nostalgic Sauganash trail became today's LaGrange Road, and like two other popular routes stemming from Archer Road, led into the verdant Palos glens and forests, where the first settlers came during the period between 1835 and 1838, to farm, cut timber, and breed stock.

In 1836, the population of what is new Palos Township, increases materially with the call for labor, in the construction of the Illinois and Michigan Canal, and the "canal work road" that became Archer Road. The demand for cordwood from the deep timbers of Palos brought an influx of immigrants from the eastern states, whose native homes were in Ireland, Scotland and Germany. The big woods resounded with the noise of Woodchopper's axes and their merry songs, as the giant first growth trees fell, to be transported to the city over Archer Road. The need of lumber continued in increase as poles were driven into the marshes upon which the great city by the lake was to stand; as well as for fueling the first locomotives and making their railroad ties.

The township was initially organized in 1850 as a part of the old York precinct, and given the name Trenton. But the officials soon learned that there was another Trenton nearby, so they asked one of their numbers, Mr. Melanchan Powell to choose a new name. It had been the tradition of the Powell family that one of their Welsh ancestors was among the sailors who made up the crew when Columbus set sail from Palos, Spain, on the great expedition. Thus the name of Palos was adopted, symbolizing the spirit of that great adventure and discovering a new world for freedom and liberty. The name also suggests the spirit of the early settlers who came among the "green hills" adjoining early Archer Road.

When the Civil War broke out, the old Mahaffey school on 135th Street, became a recruiting station where two companies were formed, leaving their crops to the care of the equally brave women. When they returned their ranks were thinned and battle-scarred, but they engaged their attention to their farming and stock raising, in their second growth timberlands, used chiefly for grazing, with an occasional giant oak reminding of other days. Their livestock drives were led from Palos over three arterial roads branching into Archer Road, and then onto the distant city. The most established of these is presently called LaGrange Road or 96th Avenue. The resourcefulness of the farmers in the Palos Township grew steadily, asking legislators conscious of its commercial contribution to the city of Chicago. In 1865, the 24th General Assembly passed an act that magnified the importance of Archer Road, and a second arterial road from it that led to the Palos settlement, now called Harlem Avenue. The legislative act read; "An Act To Locate A State Road In The County Of Cook", "The road commencing at the junction of Archer Road with the Blue Island Place Road (Western Avenue), in front of the Brighton House, near the city of Chicago, thence southwesterly along about eight miles to the Calumet Feeder (Sag canal), on the range line between the towns of Worth and Palos (Harlem Avenue), thence south on said range line across the Feeder and for a distance of about one mile, then south bearing west across the Sag swamp to a point eighty rods west of the southeast corner of section twenty-four, town of Palos, and there terminating." The now state road, integrating portions of Archer Road and Harlem Avenue, started at Chicago's southwest city limits and ended in Palos, two blocks west of 119th and Harlem Avenue.

The third arterial road of early importance in Palos Township, is today's Kean Avenue, that ended as it intersected with Archer Road. It was named for Harry F. Kean, a revered citizen of the early Palos settlement. From the time of the Civil War, Palos had been the home of the theatre. Kean, affectionately called "Pop", and his wife Bessie Cleveland Kean, were the first of their profession to come. Mr. Kean had a long career on the stage, playing in the cast with Richard Mansfield, when the latter was beginning his stage career. "Pop" fought with the North in the Civil War and carried his battle scars until his death at more than ninety years of age. He was one of the most interesting of men and one of the most cheerful. Mrs. Kean, on one or two occasions played in local short sketches, and one who heard her rich mellow tone could never forget them, nor her finished stage presence. In her prime, in London, she had supported Charlotte Cushman. During the early 1890's, Palos had acquired a colony of theatre people, as the sleek cattle gradually grew fewer. Less and less could be seen drinking from the cool spring fed streams, or on its grassy slopes. City-weary nature lovers came to buy their small estates to build their dream home in verdant Palos, transforming the present rural community into a beautiful provincial locale, bounded by charming lanes and winding roads, leading to nostalgic Archer Road.

Chapter 37: Archer Road Stage Coaches

The history of transportation over Archer Road, shared in man's continual aspirations to improve communication from the time his body was shackled down to a small radius, hampered by muddy trails, thick woods, dense marshes and hostile tribes. But his mind gave him no peace, it suggested means of travel, modes of conveyance, and, not satisfied with the development of any particular state of transportation, spurred him on and on, to the perfection of more efficient methods, to higher developments in the factors of speed, safety, comfort, carrying capacity, economy, regularity, and dependability. And down through the years, each phase of improved transportation on Archer Road were confronted with skeptics who scoffed at each proposed advance.

The first stage coaches over Archer Road came many years after the initial four wheeled coach was used by Emperor Friedrich Barbarossa of Germany in 1474 or 1475. Chicago historian, Andreas wrote of the new, local innovation, stating; "The Archer Road was the first laid out through the (Summit) settlement, and over it the stages of Dr. John Taylor Temple in the Spring of 1834, and subsequently those of Frink and Walker used to travel toward Juliet-now Joliet and Galena. To stand in this old tavern (nw. cor. Archer and Harlem avenues) and re-people the scene with old inhabitants, to imagine the limbering stages on their way to Ottawa, via Lockport and Juliet, dashing up with all the jingling of harness and prancing, of steeds attendant upon the "Rockets" speed of ten miles an hour, and in fancy to hear the passengers discoursing of the transaction in the town of Chicago."

Andreas was premature in stating that the stages passed over that segment of Archer Road from Summit to Lockport in 1834. That portion of the road was not improved by Colonel Archer in conjunction with digging the adjoining Illinois and Michigan canal until 1836. It is more than likely that before that segment of Archer Road was improved, the stage coaches crossed the Desplaines River in Summit, and followed the old Chicago trail to Joliet, so vividly described by the by the early settler, A. Van Dyke Pierson, who wrote: "The story of the highway from Bloomington to Chicago started in 1831. The road ran along the west side of the Desplaines, forty or fifty miles, crossing over the east side at Summit, continuing on the east side, passing through Brighton, and entered Chicago at Archer Avenue, then known as Archer Road." Once the "canal road" was completed between Summit and Lockport, the stage coaches traversed over the improved route, as substantiated by historian Bessie Pierce, who wrote; "One of the most important of these roads was that which led to the southwest. Formerly laid out as the "Canal Road" and following the line of the old portage road, that had been bridged at the Chicago portage it crossed the Sauganash Swamps in the old Sag outlet, and continued to Joliet. From there it ran to Ottawa, thence Peru and Peoria, where it joined with roads to St Louis and Springfield."

Archer Road's early importance as a stage route was also acknowledged by William Le Baron Jr, who published his "History of Will County" in 1878, although his dates seemed to erroneous. He wrote; "In 1838 the canal cut a road direct to Chicago, which bears off to the right of the Chicago and Alton, and in 1839, the road was opened through from Chicago to Ottawa, which afterwards became quite famous as a stage route. It used to be a great thoroughfare of travel when stage coaches were the common mode of transit." An early reference to the stage service over Archer Road appeared in the Chicago

American newspaper, August 6, 1836, that read; "John Temple & Co. are proprietors of a stage line from Chicago to Peoria", that, "the through trip is made in two days—to Ottawa the first day", that "the stage leaves Chicago at four in the morning arrives in Juliet (Joliet) at two" and, "seats can be taken at Markle's Exchange Coffee House." The name Joliet did not officially supersede Juliet until 1845. The earliest Archer stage schedule was "three times each week in 1836. By 1848, a daily stage, except Sundays was maintained between Chicago and Springfield, through Ottawa, Peru and Peoria." By 1849, the Illinois state capital had been moved from Vandalia to Springfield and during a span of thirteen years, before the state capital and Chicago were joined by the first railroad in 1852, many of the Chicagoland legislators traversed between these points over the Archer stage route.

The stage contract to carry the mail between Chicago and Ottawa was acquired by Fr. John Temple, a pious and earnest Baptist Christian. He had arrived in Chicago early in July 1835, coming from Washington D.C., with a contract to carry mails from Chicago to Fort Howard (Green Bay). His contract gave him surety of a living, so that his surplus energy could be used in the service of the Lord. The American newspaper of April 1, 1837 stated that Dr. Temple "had sold his stage line" to Frink and Walker, who for years enjoyed a practical monopoly of passenger transportation over a large portion of the Middle West. John Frink was thus experienced when in 1836, he migrated to Chicago. In the following year, he purchased Temple's route over Archer Road. One of his employees William Beckman, reminiscing in 1914, in Sacramento, California, where he became a banker after leaving Chicago in 1852, wrote of driving a Frisk and Walker stage coach over the nostalgic Archer route as a young man. "I drove for two winters, when the canal was frozen up, from Chicago to Joliet, which was all night work both ways. They used to put us young drivers at the night work, as our eye sight was better that the old men. The stage horses of that time were worth $100.00 a piece, and instead of raising race horses, they would raise stage horses, because the stage company always had good horses, good harnesses, good coaches, and everything up to date."

Historian Andreas revealed the half-way station between Chicago and Joliet, when he wrote: "The first house built in Summit was the stage ranche on the location of the hotel now (1884) kept by Dennis O'Brian, erected by Russell K. Heacock about 1838. Other narrators state that the ranche was built by the stage company about 1835, and subsequently bought by Heacock." The exploits of this colorful person are synonymous with the early history of Archer Road, up and down its route, from Bridgeport of Summit. He was born in Connecticut in 1781, and licensed as an attorney in the Indian Territory in 1808, that also encompassed the present state of Illinois. Heacock came to Fort Dearborn in 1827, and shortly thereafter, made residence at the Forks of the South Branch of the Chicago River, adjoining Archer Road. The site became a landmark called Heacock's Point. In 1830, he claimed all the land bounded by West 31st Street, South Halsted Street, West 39th Street, and South Ashland Avenue, today's community of Bridgeport. His name appeared during the state election held August 2, 1830, when thirty-two voters from Chicago exercised their privilege, and one of the election judges was Heacock. In the following year, he acquired the first of three licenses granted by the newly organized Cook County that on April 13, 1831, allowed him to "keep a tavern at his residence." Five months later, Hancock was appointed the first of four justices of the peace. In June 1832, he was re-named as viewer, and selected the present route of Archer Road, as the new Cook County highway leading from Chicago to Hickory Creek. The activities of Heacock had no end. In July 1835, the first recorded larceny case involving a theft of $34.00 was heard by Squire Heacock. He was also present at the historical meeting that took place August 10, 1838, convened to debate incorporating the town of Chicago. As the justice of the peace, he administered the oath. The measure was passed, but Heacock was the only one to dissent, since his residence at Heacock's Point was outside the newly established limits of the town of Chicago. In 1835, he came into possession of the eighty acres of land at the junction of Archer Road and Western Avenue, which after his death, became the site of the thriving Brighton livestock center for many years. He was also a strong advocate for construction the Illinois and Michigan canal, from his residence at Heacock's Point. At one point when it seemed that the project was to be abandoned for financial reasons, he pleaded, wrote, and spoke for the more economical "shallow out." Once the change he advocated was made, he became known as the "father of the shallow out."

Russell K. Heacock build or purchased the stage coach ranche at Archer and Harlem avenues, sometime around 1858, adjoining his farm retreat some two miles south, is the present suburb of Bridgeview. He was credited with building the first bridge across the Desplaines River in Summit, connecting the Old Chicago Trail with Archer Road. Heacock was a resident of the city of Chicago when the cholera epidemic struck in 1849. He fled with his wife and two sons to his farm in Bridgeview to escape the disease. They were all stricken and died in quick succession between the 28th and 30th of June 1849. They were buried on the farm site, later called the Old Brown farm, that was owned by William Brown, familiarly designated at "Old Scotch".

Just how long the stage route continued over Archer Road is difficult to say, but the stage ranche at Archer and Harlem avenues, was still in operation in 1845, with Thomas Dutcher as proprietor, who in the fall of that year turned it over to Dennis O'Brian. It is more than likely that stage coaches over Archer Road declined in popularity with the introduction of the plank roads in 1848, and the building of the adjoining Chicago and Alton railroad in 1857. Recorded for posterity are three particular narratives that are charming in their description of stage travel over the Archer route in 1837, 1840 and in 1846. The earliest recorded episode of travel in 1837 evolved around America's greatest orator, Daniel Webster. Toward the close of Presidents Jackson's administration, Webster was disappointed over the course of political events, and planned to terminate his public career and begin life anew as a farmer on the prairies of Illinois. He purchased a thousand acres of land near LaSalle, and set his son Fletcher to develop the estate. The project never materialized but Webster's interest in the western country let him to embark in the spring of 1837 upon an extensive tour as far west as St Louis. From this point he began his return east by way of Chicago, first paying a visit to his incipient estate near LaSalle, which he had named Salisbury in honor of his New Hampshire birthplace. He left St Louis, June 14, traveling over the Archer Road as he neared Chicago, at the close of that month. On his approach, the joyful townsmen went out in a great cavalcade, ten miles to the Desplaines, to escort him into the city. Before the Lake House he made an address on the issues of the day, and on July 1st, he left Chicago by boat for Michigan City, where he took up the stage journey to Detroit.

In 1840, Mrs. Eliza Steele essayed her "Summer Journey in the West", that described her adventure over the Archer stage trail. She and her husband left Chicago, after purchasing passage to Peoria, with bed and board included for the sum of eleven dollars each. The stage left the city limits over Archer Road at nine o'clock at night, and a twenty-four ride brought the travelers to Peru, where the steam boat Frontier was waiting to receive them. According to schedule, they should have reached Peoria early in the morning, but a heavy fog held up the boat, and breakfast time found them many miles short of the destination. At Peoria, the Chicago line terminated and the travelers were delayed awaiting the arrival of a boat for St Louis.

The hazards of traveling by stage over Archer Road were vividly described by William Cullen Bryant, traveler of much experience, having journeyed to all parts of the world. But he lacked the courage to encounter a second stage coach journey between Chicago and Ottawa after his ordeal in 1846. And on his return journey he hired a private conveyance. His complaints against the public stage was that the vehicle was built like the English post-coach, set high upon springs, which he considered absurd for the roads of Illinois. It seemed to be set too high in the air in order that it might more easily overturn. During his eighty-five mile trip, he narrowly escaped as many as a dozen times when the stage overturned. But during one of those catastrophes' he failed to escape. The stage had left Chicago in the morning, traveling over Archer Road, and toward sunset was about to cross for the second or third time the channel of the Illinois and Michigan canal below Mount Joliet.

At this point Bryant wrote; "There had once been a bridge at the crossing place, but the water had risen in the canal, and the timbers and planks had floated away, leaving only the stones which formed the foundation. In attempting to ford the channel, the blundering driver came too near the bridge, the coach wheels on one side rose upon the stones, and in the other, sank deep into the mud, and we were overturned in an instant. The outside passengers were pitched head-foremost into the canal, and four of those within were lying under water.

We extricated ourselves as well as we could, the men waded out, the women were carried, and when we got to shore, it was found that although drenched with water, and plastered with mud, nobody was either drowned or hurt."

"A farm wagon passing at the moment, forded the canal without the least difficulty, and taking the female passengers, conveyed them to the next farmhouse, about a mile distant. We got out the baggage, which was completely soaked with water, set up the carriage on its wheels, in doing which we had to stand waist high in the mud and water, and reached the hospitable farmhouse about half past nine o'clock. Its owner was an emigrant from Kinderhook on the Hudson, who claimed to be a Dutchman and a Christian, and I had no reason to doubt that he was either. His kind family made us free of their house and we passed the night in drying ourselves and getting our baggage ready to proceed the next day." The second day of travel over the especially rough road brought the stage coach to Peru late in the night, the remainder of which the travelers spent in an inn on the bank of the river, listening to the mosquitoes. In the light of the writers experience it is perhaps little wonder that he declined to again venture over the perilous stage route that included the thirty mile length of the Archer Road. He went to great lengths to warn all travelers between Chicago and Peru, exposing the stage agent who promised a journey of sixteen hours, when "double that number would be nearer the truth."

Chapter 38: The Omnibus to the Canal House

The earliest local transportation over Archer Road for the public, came in the form of a modified stage coach in 1859. These unique omnibuses had served adequately in Chicago's business district for many years. They were usually built with the seats running lengthwise of the body, and the entrance was at the rear. The driver sat on a raised seat projecting from the front of the body. The omnibuses were elaborately decorated and were often named after some celebrity. At first it was the practice of having a boy collect fares at the rear entrance. This was dropped and the money was deposited by passengers in a box besides the driver's seat. Change up to two dollars was supposed to be furnished by the driver on request. This was passed back to the passenger in an envelope through a small hole in the roof. Since the driver could not see into the interior of the omnibus, it was necessary to have a special arrangement to signal him when to start or stop. This was done by means of a strap running from the rear door to the driver's leg. A pull on the strap indicated that the door was being opened by someone who wanted to get off or on. A slack strap indicated that the door was closed. The newly initiated service led from Chicago's business district by way of State Street and Archer Road to the door of the historical Canal House in Bridgeport, the thriving scene of transient customers, mule skinners, teamsters, canal captains and their crews. The innovation was recorded for posterity in the Chicago-Press Tribune of Thursday, August 4, 1859, which read; "A new line of omnibuses are to ply on the Archer Road from State Street to Bridgeport. It will be a great convenience, especially as the Canal Office is located there."

Chapter 39: Horse Drawn Street Cars

As the local omnibus service was being initiated over Archer Road to Bridgeport in 1859, Chicago, Pittsburgh and Cincinnati joined the ranks of cities having horse-drawn street railways. Six years passed before the horse cars drawn over tracks replaced the Archer omnibus, when tracks were laid on Archer Road from Stewart Avenue (400 west) to State Street. From this point they proceeded into the business district via State, Lake, Wabash and Randolph streets, then returned south over State Street and southwest on Archer Road. The line was extended to Fuller Avenue (1300 west) in the memorable year of 1865, when the Civil Was ceased, and President Abraham Lincoln was assassinated.

There were many different truck designs in those early horse-car days. They were mostly flat strips of wrought iron, and were laid in short lengths on wooded stringers resting on cross-ties, spaced about five feet apart. It was not until after the introduction of the steel rail of much greater depth and strength that the stringers were eliminated and the rails laid directly on the cross-ties. At one time there was an idea that the lead of the rail should be on the inside and the flange of the wheel on the outside. This arrangement was the direct opposite of steam railroad practice, but its advocates contended that it was more satisfactory for the other vehicles using the streets. The best shape for the rail was another matter of controversy, but this was never settled until after the horse-car had passed out of the transportation picture.

The most serious of the operating problems centered in the horse himself. Some of the larger street railways had a thousand or more of them. A good animal for this kind of work cost about one hundred and twenty five dollars. This was less that the cost of a car, which averaged around seven hundred and fifty dollars. But it was necessary to have several shifts of horses for each car, so the total investment in animals was usually greater than that in equipment. As a matter of fact, an early report of the American Street Railway Association stated that about forty percent of the entire investment of the average company was in horses and stables.

The interior of the horse-drawn street cars had a single compartment with seats running lengthwise on both sides of a center aisle. The upholstered seats could accommodate from twenty-four to thirty passengers. Doors connected the car interior with platforms at the front and rear, one for the driver and one for the conductor. The car roof extended over these platforms, and they were provided with low metal dashboards, but otherwise they were entirely open, assuring the car crew of plenty of fresh air in all weather. Some of the smaller cars had no rear platforms, but only a step from the rear door to the ground. They were called bob-tails."

Oil lamps illuminated the car interior at night. These lamps were often rather smoky, a characteristic which aggravated the ventilating problem. Two tons was the weight of the ordinary horse-car, and the passengers weighed another two tons. For this, companies used two horses per car. The chief objection against the "bob-tail" cars was the trouble in depositing the fare in the box at the forward end of the car. It was more or less difficult, especially for ladies to maintain an equilibrium. The attached horse furnished all the moving power and most of the stopping power. Their efforts to stop was supplemented by a system of brakes which the driver applied by turning a goose-necked handle on a vertical staff attached to the dash-board. Watching the winding and unwinding of this handle was one of the most entertaining features of riding the Archer horse-cars, and was rivaled only by the fun of listening to the clang of the bells, the little bell. By which the conductor signaled the driver to start or stop, and the big bell, by which the driver warned pedestrians and other vehicles out of the way of his prancing steeds. The initial car barn servicing the Archer cars and stabling the horses was erected at the junction of State Street and Archer Road in 1859. When it burned down in 1877, a new one was constructed on Archer Road at Pitney Court (1500 west) in Bridgeport, and remained in service until it was abandoned in 1908.

Chapter 40: Cable Cars

The 1880's were the great years of the horse-car business, but it was to some degree the pride that goes before the fall. The serious competitors of the horse railway had arisen. One was the cable railway, and the other was the electric railway. The end of the horse-car era was in sight. Although cable cars were never installed on Archer Road they became a counterpart in transporting Archer riders into the business district from the junction at State Street. At this point the horses were unfastened from the Archer cars, and the vehicle was attached to the State Street cable car in tandem. Dating back to 1882 this service proceeded into the business district via State, Lake, Wabash, and Randolph streets, returning south to Archer Road, where the horses were again attached to the car for the trip southwestward to Fuller avenue in Bridgeport.

The new innovation consisted of a gripping clamp on the cable car, extending downward through a slot in the pavement that would take hold or let go the moving cable, at the will of the driver or "gripman." Brakes similar to those on horse cars were provided to stop the vehicle after the grip on the cable had been released. The speed ranged from six to eight miles an hour in the business district, and twelve to fourteen miles an hour in residential areas. At the height of the cable cars success, Chicago had four times as many trailers than grip cars. The system had many advantages over the horse-drawn cars. It contributed to the cleanliness and health of the city. It eliminated the problem of removing from the street the voiding of two or three thousand horses, while the constant clatter of hoofs on the pavement was supplemented by the quiet gliding of a train, scarcely audible from the sidewalk. The cable car proved its prowess in the winter, being excellent snow fighters.

On more than one occasion when all the steam railroads entering the city of Chicago were tied up for hours by a heavy snowfall, the cable cars were running as usual, and their tracks afforded the only path of travel for pedestrians and teams.

Cable car operation was no child's play. The machinery required to keep miles of cable running smoothly over the rollers under the pavement was vast and complicated. The proper operation of the grip was extremely difficult. A "gripman" had to be one of strong physique, well trained and careful to follow instructions. He needed plenty of muscle and skill to manipulate the grip lever so that the car would not start too suddenly. This was particularly true when the cable was new and had not worn to a smooth surface. He had to know his line. There were many places, such as crossings and switches, where the cable had to be released and grasped again at exactly the right time. Sometimes a loose strand of the underground cable would become wrapped around the grip of the car, so that it could not be released by the driver. Then the car just kept on going, the spectacle of a car dashing unchecked along the street at a speed of eleven or twelve miles an hour, frightened many passengers who resided down Archer Road. The car could be halted only when the conductor jumped to the pavement, found one of the infrequent telephones of those days, and called the power house just beyond the junction of Archer Road on State Street, to stop the cable.

Chapter 41: Horse Railway Extended

Exactly nineteen years elapsed before the Archer horse-drawn railway was extended one mile from Bridgeport to Chicago's city limits at Western boulevard (2400 west), adjoining the town of Brighton. The historical event was recorded in the Town of Lake Vindicator newspaper, dated Saturday, August 8, 1884, which read; "Three trial runs on the new Brighton extension of the Archer Avenue horse-car railroad was made on Tuesday last and Wednesday morning, regular trips were commenced. The first car left the barn at Bridgeport at 5:48 am and returned at 6:06 am, making the round trip in 36 minutes. Trips will be made every twelve minutes and continue until 11 o'clock in the evening. The first car that came up on Monday morning ran off the switch at Brighton, owing to the rails being too close together, causing the wheels to mount the rails and running off. The avenue was muddy and present cars cannot be reached from the sidewalks in Brighton. A wooded platform or a crossing should be build. The Brighton terminus is opposite Nugent's saloon at 3696 Archer avenue. The cars are rather small and without cushions." Other references to the new extension in later editions of the Vindicator newspaper read; "the tracks were a new innovation and the powder wagons find the car tracks very useful", "The teamsters wheel their vehicles upon them and avoid being stuck." In 1887, the horse railway was extended to Pershing Road (2600 west), just prior to the electrification of the whole Archer route.

Chapter 42: The Hissing Trolley

Chicago put the first electric trolley car into operation in 1880, sometime after a Belgian sculptor, Charles J. VanDepoele, had been experimenting with the use of electricity as a mode of transportation here in the United States. It was not until 1894 before the Archer route was electrified from State Street to Pershing road. At first the cars were quite short in length and were carried on a single frame or truck, mounted on four wheels. Seats were provided for about twenty passengers per car if they expected to keep their budgets in balance. That meant larger cars, but the limit of length with a four wheel car was soon reached. If the axles were placed too far apart the car could not go around the sharp curves, such as existed at the Archer terminals. The car builders solved this problem with a body supported by two independent four-wheel trucks, pivoted near the ends of the car. The J. G Brill Company, veteran car builders for the street railway industry designed the first double-truck electric car. They had seats for about thirty-six passengers, and their lengths were gradually increases upwards to forty seats.

In 1896 the Archer electric trolley was extended down the road to Kostner Avenue (4400 west), and in 1900, it reached the city limits at Cicero avenue (4800 west). This was the furthest penetration southwestward over Archer Road by any Chicago franchised railway. From this terminus was initiated an interurban trolley service that ran to distant Joliet for many years. Long gone is the nostalgic depot that stood on the southwest corner of Archer Road and Cicero Avenue, that accommodated passengers transferring to and from the city trolley and the country interurban.

Chapter 43: The Awesome Interurban

In review, public transportation over the full thirty mile length of Archer Road was first initiated back in 1836, and continued until the railroads replaced the stage coach during the 1850's. Gradually, the city of Chicago extended local service in 1859, with an omnibus running from the business district, down Archer Road to Ashland Avenue (1400 west) at Bridgeport. This was followed by the horse drawn street cars, that reached as far as Pershing road (2600 west) by 1887. Eventually, the route was electrified, with Chicago trolley cars making their furthest extension southwestward to the early city limits at Cicero Avenue in 1900. These were the heydays of the trolley street railways, as companies across the country merged to form huge interurban systems. In Connecticut, a street railway system had more than 800 miles of track and served virtually every important city from Boston to New York in 1918. One could go from New York to Chicago by electric railway in those days. That involved the use of some lines that were not trolleys in the ordinary sense, but rather electric interurban railways. In 1899, this new mode of transportation restored public service over the full length of Archer Road once again, when the Chicago and Joliet Electric Railway Company laid their tracks from Joliet to the Chicago trolley terminus depot at Cicero Avenue.

How well I remember that awesome country trolley, that swayed over its tracks, hidden by the high grasses on both sides of the Archer thoroughfare. Many of my boyhood escapades during the twenties, evolved around the Archer trolley car barn, located at Pershing Road and Rockwell Street, where hours were spent playing motorman or conductor with friends, intrigued with the sound of the driver's floor bell, and the hissing of his lever, that sifted sand onto the tracks below. I was familiar with the variously designed trolley's kept there, but only the awesome interurban that ran outside the city limits could move me to ecstasy. The infrequent opportunity to ride that majestic conveyance only came when my widowed mother took me in hand to visit the grave of my deceased father in Resurrection Cemetery, located on Archer Road in Justice Park, Illinois. Riding the city trolley to the depot at Cicero Avenue, was always uneventful, subdued by the exhilarated anticipation of soon boarding the "country trolley." Soon our trolley approached Cicero Avenue, entering the intersection, and following the sweeping curve of the tracks to the depot set back off the southwest corner of Archer and Cicero avenues. Only the firm grip of my mother's hand prevented me from jumping off the slowly moving car, so as to hasten into the large rambling building that served as the transfer station, separating city and country.

Once inside the depot, an atmosphere of a railroad station prevailed, a scene to enliven any boy. People were standing at the ticket window, purchasing interurban tickets from the agent seated behind the barred window. Others remained seated on the long wooden benches, waiting for interurban trolley to make its appearance. My anxiety was appeased to a degree only when mother capitulated to my pleas made at the candy display. Then out in the distance would come the mellow whistle of the interurban. With mother in hand we moved through the swinging doors on the west side of the depot, and awaited the "country trolley" to make its wide turn over its own tracks and approach the station. It was an awesome thing, as it rumbled arrogantly over its private right-of-way, with the suppressed power of a locomotive, easing up, with its big flaring cowcatchers grimacing dangerously. Once the car stopped, and the motorman opened the door, mother released the grip on my hand, exploiting my maneuvering ability to squirm through the waiting crowd and capture a vacant seat with an advantageous view of the countryside. The interior of the interurban seemed a marvel of luxury to a youngster, who was more familiar with the stiff basket woven upholstered seats of the city trolley's, as compared to the country car's seats finished in rich green plush.

Up front the motorman checked his air gauges, then grabbed hold of the rope hanging stretched that gave out a "toot", then slowly and heavily the car crept out from the depot and crossed over to the north side of Archer Road, swinging onto its private right-of-way in the high grass, running parallel to the paved road. Steadily he notched up his controller until the handle was against its stop. The continuing acceleration of the car was astonishing; it went faster and faster until you were secretly afraid it might leave the rails. The poles at the side track seemed to stream past like fence posts, and out the rear there was a tremendous swirl of dust and cinders. Beneath the floor the motor gave a steady, rising hum as background to the click of rail joints and the hiss of the trolley on the overhead wire. Everywhere you saw the details of true railroading, as we approached the junction with Roberts Road (8000 west), the site of the Chicago and Elgin "car barn". Signaling our presence, the motorman reached for the cord and gave out with a melodious "toot", "toot", and seconds later we cleared the many switches and were again in open country. Long since leaving the Cicero avenue depot, I had abandoned mother to explore the rear of the car. Since the front of the car was used as the entrance and exit, the motorman also served as conductor. What attracted me to the rear of the car, was the small but unique stove, with its stove pipe protruding through the roof. This was the only source of heat in the winter maintained by the ambidextrous motorman. Our destination always came too soon, signaled by the frantic waving of my mother's hand as she called me back to her seat. Seconds later our car came to a hissing stop in front of the Resurrection cemetery entrance. After alighting hesitantly, I long fully watched my interurban speed through the countryside, swaying in the deep cuts as it disappeared in the horizon. The Archer interurban service from Cicero avenue to Joliet, initiated in 1899, came to a halt in 1938. The cause might well have seemed unbelievable then. Who could have taken seriously the wheezy flivvers, or the chain driven, hard tired trucks and busses? How was it possible to respect these slow and erratic contrivances when the kingly interurban, its whistle blowing, could scatter them so contemptuously at every crossing encounter. C.C. Duncan in reminiscence of the late interurbans, wrote: "Today the old roadbed, like an Indian mound, winds down through the woodlands; the rails, wire, and the ties are long ago sold: the embankments are crumbled; and gone forever from the valley is the mellow whistle of the interurban."

Chapter 44: Contemporary Archer Buses

Public acceptance of the bus as a mode of transportation had come a long way before its initial introduction on Archer Road in 1938. The first challenge to the street trolley by a gas driven, rubber tire car came in Los Angeles on July 1, 1914. They were "jitneys", a name bestowed upon these vehicles because of their five cent fare. The name became a way of referring to five cents worth of anything. The jitney bus was not the first common carrier motor vehicle in American cities. Credit for taking the initial step belongs to the Fifth Avenue Coach Company in New York City, which imported and put on their route in 1905, a single, twenty-four passenger double-decked motorbus. In 1922, street railway companies began buying busses, which increased greatly two years later, by the elimination of the mechanical gear shift to an electric drive. Fundamentally, the gas-electric principle was simply this; a gasoline engine was directly connected to an electric generator. This generator provided electric currant for electric motors, which drove the rear wheels. Into the scrap heap went the gear shift, with its tremendous wear and tear upon the bus, and the strain upon the driver. Along with the gear shift went the grinding gears, the jerking, as the bus slammed from one speed to another. Then came the hydraulic transmission in 1939.

The common carrier bus had come a long way when the Chicago and Joliet Electric Railway Company abandoned their Archer Road interurban service from Cicero avenue to Joliet in 1938. The company transferred to busses, but terminated operations a few years later. In 1934, the Chicago Transit Authority placed the first Archer bus into service, which in reality was an extension line from the city trolley terminus at Cicero avenue to Harlem avenue (7200 west). In the meantime the Bluebird Bus Company of Lyons, Illinois, initiated bus service from Chicago's downtown business district that ran to Joliet via Randolph, Odgen, Cermak, Cicero, 63rd, and Archer Road. The contemporary Chicago busses finally replaced the last Archer trolley in 1948, and extended the route to its present terminus at Harlem Avenue.

Chapter 45: William Beatty Archer

Gleanings of Archer Road would not be complete without reviewing the dedicated life of Colonel William Beatty Archer, for whom the thoroughfare was named back in 1836. His many deeds during a long life have been obscured and gone unheralded in the Chicagoland area, primarily because of his intimacy with his native region in east-central Illinois, 120 miles south of Chicago. His father, Zachariah Archer was born in the county of Downs, Ireland in 1708. He came to America when twenty years old, and during the Revolutionary War he enlisted from Northumberland County, Pennsylvania in 1776, with Captain William Pebbles of the Pennsylvania rifle regime, commanded by Colonel Samuel Miles. Zachariah was transferred to the Pennsylvania State regiment with Captain Matthew Scott and Colonel Walter Stewart. He was in the battle of Long Island, Trenton, and Brandywine, and was in camp at Valley Forge.

After the war he migrated to Warren County, Ohio, where in 1791 his son, William Beatty Archer was born, the oldest of eight children. Young Archer was taken to Kentucky at an early age, and from there to Illinois, landing in 1817 in a keel boat. This event took place during a memorable Wabash river freshet, when the family landed on the site that later became known as the Block House School in southern Clark County, Illinois. Zachariah Archer died in 1822 and was buried in Walnut Prairie cemetery, at the age of seventy.

Although William Archer pursued the avocation of a farmer, he was a civil engineer, and became one of the most important and influential men in east-central Illinois. The people recognized his sterling qualities, and he at once took a commanding position in the affairs of the infant settlement. He did more for Clark County than any man in his day, but no recognition was given him for his long and valuable service until after his death in 1870. He erected the town of Marshall, 190 miles south of Chicago in 1835, and during its centennial, Main street was renamed Archer avenue to perpetuate his memory. A year after Illinois became a state, the legislature approved an Act on March 22, 1819, creating new county divisions. William Archer was appointed the first County and Circuit Clerk of Clark County, that not only encompassed west-central Illinois, but present Cook County as well. He resigned the former office in 1820, and the latter 1822. William became an anti-slavery candidate for the state legislature against an opponent William Lowery, a member of the Third General Assembly, which adjourned February 10, 1823. Archer was triumphantly elected by a vote of one hundred and thirty-five to five. This was his first state office, and at the age of thirty –one years, he became a member of the Fourth General Assembly (1824-26),which convened at the early state capital at Vandalia, November 15, 1824 In1826,Archer was elected to the state senate and served two terms, covering the Fifth, Sixth, Seventh and Eighth Assemblies (1822-34).

At the outbreak of the Black Hawk War in 1838, William Archer recruited the first company of Mounted Volunteers at Darwin Illinois and was elected Captain. Upon arrival at headquarters, Captain Archer was assigned to the staff of the commanding general, with the rank of Colonel. He was thus a State Senator when the Sauk War broke out, and like his friend, Abraham Lincoln, a member of the militia. After the Indian campaign, Colonel Archer was an unsuccessful candidate for Lieutenant-Governor in 1834. He was always absorbed in projects of public improvement. The controlling idea of his life was for the improvement and development of his country, state and town. Colonel Archer and his intimate associate, Governor

Joseph Duncan founded the county seat of Marshall in Clark County. The first public notice that the Colonel intended laying out the town at the crossing of the National Road, one of the earliest turnpikes across the Alleghany mountains, at the junction with the Vincennes and Chicago State Road, was made in the form of a printed circular under the heading, "Internal Improvements", and dated January 20, 1835. The firm of Cole and Cole of Marshall, has preserved one of the original circulars that contains the following excerpts; "Joseph Duncan and William B. Archer, having purchased the land on the National Road, where Vincennes and Chicago State Road crosses paid National Road in Clark County, and intending to lay out the town there as soon as practicable." On September 23, 1835, Colonel Archer issued a circular announcing the approaching sale of lots therein "situated ten miles from Darwin, fifteen miles south of Peoria, fifty miles from Danville, and sixteen miles from Terre Haute."

Colonel Archer's friend and business associate, Joseph Duncan, was indirectly associated in the cause of Daniel Pope Cook's death, for whom Cook County was named and who authorized the construction of the Illinois and Michigan canal, whose by-product was the improved Archer Road. Most ironically, Duncan defeated incumbent Cook for his congressional seat, contributing to his early death in 1837. Duncan went on to become governor of Illinois and appointed his associate, William Archer to supervise the digging of the canal that Daniel Cook had made a reality by his legislative skill. Back in 1824, the presidential election winner had to be decided in the House of Representatives. Illinois had chosen Andrew Jackson, but Illinois legislator, Daniel Pope Cook cast his for Adams, and the resentment against him at home was very strong. When Cook ran for re-election, he was shocked in to losing to a political unknown at the time, Joseph Duncan. Also shocked were the men who voted against Cook. "We did not intend to defeat little Cook", they said, "but only to lessen his majority, so as to make him feel his dependence on us." But inadvertently, they had killed him by this political defeat. This frail, but handsome person had lived on vitality, and before the year was out, charming little Cook was dead at the age of thirty-three, largely attributed to a broken heart.

By 1834, Joseph Duncan's political stature had grown to where he was elected governor of Illinois. One of his official acts created the third State Board of Canal Commissioners, February 10, 1835, to which he appointed as commissioners; Colonel William Beatty Archer, Colonel Gurdon Hubbard and General William Thornton. In his specific capacity as the acting commissioner, Colonel Archer came to the Chicagoland area to supervise the digging of the canal, and build the canal road that later was named in his honor. His appointment terminated March 3, 1837, where upon he returned to his home in Marshall, and became engrossed in promoting various state roads and railroad enterprises. He practically rebuilt the Vincennes and Chicago Road from Darwin to Marshall at his expense. He was one of the prime advocates that resulted in the Marshall and Charleston Road becoming a state road in 1837. In 1838, the Colonel was re-elected to the House of Representatives, serving in the Eleventh, Twelfth and Fifteenth General Assemblies. He thus accumulated eight years in both the State Senate and House, covering a period from 1884 to 1846. He served two terms, the Eleventh and Twelfth, in the House of Representatives with Abraham Lincoln, which doubtlessly was the commencement of their mutual admiration and friendship. When William Archer was a delegate to the first Republican convention at Philadelphia in 1836, he enthusiastically supported Lincoln's candidacy for the office of vice-president, and was the first to bring his name to public notice. This was revealed in a letter of his, retained by the

Chicago Historical Society, that reads; "I slated A. Lincoln for vice president on the evening of the 18th after dark, and it took well."

Chapter 46: Untarnished Legacy

When Illinois called for volunteers during the Mexican War, Colonel Archer raised a company of seventy-five men, and started from Marshall, June 6, 1846, in wagons. Arriving in Alton, they reported to the governor of the state, and were received as Company No. 27, June 9th. They served eighteen days and were discharged, June 27th, the state's quota having been filled by previously accepted troops. In 1849, he was again elected Circuit Clerk, serving until 1852. In 1854, Archer was an Anti-Nebraskan Whig candidate for Congress, in opposition to James C. Allen of Palestine, Crawford County. The results were very close, although Judge Allen received the certificate of election. The Colonel contested his right to the seat, with the result that Congress declared the seat vacant and referred the question back to the people. In a new election held August 1856, Archer was defeated, and thereafter held no public office after that date, other than being a delegate to the Republican Convention in 1856. This brought to a close a record of thirty-three years of almost continuous service as a county and state official.

Colonel Archer's dedication to projects of public improvement made him careless as to his private affairs, and nearly lost everything he owned. In one of these enterprises he again became associated with the Chicagoland area in an indirect manner. The railroad right-of-way, which crosses Archer Road in Chicago at Central Park Avenue (3600 west), was initially laid at ground level in 1856, by the Cincinnati, Logansport and Chicago Railroad. In his native east-central region of Illinois, Colonel Archer was one of the original promoters of the old Chicago and Vincennes Railroad, the first projected from that region to Chicago. In 1865, the name was changed to the Chicago, Danville and Vincennes Railroad, and at that time came into possession of the Chicago right-of-way that crossed Archer Road, named in his honor. Colonel Archer was also related with the construction of the old Wabash Valley Railroad, the predecessor of the present Wabash Railroad. He entered the work of this project with all the zeal and energy of his indomitable nature. He gave his time and money, and just as it seemed that success would crown his efforts, the project was abandoned. He never was destined to see its completion.

Colonel Archer's character was known to be rugged, strong, resolute, with a peculiar individuality. He had firm confidence and an abiding faith in his convictions of right and moral courage to defend them. Although raised in a slave state, the Colonel at an early age, imbibed an unconquerable aversion to human slavery, and during his long and busy life, whether in legislative halls or the private walks of life, he always advocated the cause of freedom and Free State. In private life, he was genial and kind, and around his private character, clustered many noble virtues. He was married to Eliza Harlan, and the result of that union was a daughter, who because the wife of Woodford Dulaney of Kentucky. William Archer's religious convictions were not known, but he had the reputation of an honest man. He was an honored member of the Masonic fraternity for sixty years. The Colonel was tall in stature, sparse and slightly stooped, and had the endurance of an Indian, insensible to fatigue, a man of iron. Possessed at one time of ample means, he lost almost everything by his continued involvement in public improvement schemes. He gave the land to Marshall for a Court House and a jail. Later he gave away more land, and when he died he was a very poor man. For this he labored, for this he toiled, and this he gave the best years of his manhood. Time bent his form, silvered his locks and enfeebled his steps, but it could not conquer his spirit. But at last, the end came.   Bowed down by the weight of seventy-eight years and infirmities, incurred by a long life of incessant toil for the general good, on the 9th day of August 1870 he calmly passed to his final reward.   His only legacy was an untarnished name and the enduring monuments of his labor and enterprise in the state.   The Colonel sleeps in Walnut Prairie cemetery, some ten miles south of his town of Marshall, besides his father Zachariah Archer, a soldier of the Revolutionary War.

Chapter 47: Town of Marshall

Without seeing or knowing the Colonel's distant town of Marshall, the biography of William Archer seemed incomplete. The final chapter was successfully concluded when my wife and four children accompanied me, as we left Chicago one Sunday morning in July, destined for his country town 190 miles south of our fair city. Our family car sped down Highway Route 1, adjoining the historical path first made popular in 1823 by fur trader Gurdon S. Hubbard, when it was called Hubbard's trail and the Vincennes trail. Who knew then that in 1836 Colonel Hubbard and Colonel Archer were to serve together as commissioners digging the Illinois and Michigan Canal? Some seventy-two miles along our trip, we entered the town of Watseka, named for the Indian princess Hubbard had married to strengthen his fur trading relations with her people. Another sixty-five miles brought us into Danville, where the earliest Chicagoland canal section land titles along Archer Road were recorded in the Federal land office located there.

When we finally reached our destination of Marshall, we drove into a gasoline station to replenish our supply of fuel. From the youthful attendant we learned that we were but one block short of the town's main street named Archer Avenue. The town of Marshall, with its population of 3300, had been named by Colonel Archer for his idol, Chief Justice John Marshall, of the United States Supreme Court. Its broad shady streets were bordered with fine old houses, a town with a contemporary air, as though recalling pleasant memories of the past.

The afternoon was hot and sunny, as I parked the family car at the curb on the main thoroughfare of Archer Avenue, for the express purpose of taking some pictures of the town with my camera. The business district was a peaceful sight that Sunday, its unblemished streets and immaculate buildings abandoned by the populace for the Sabbath. After leaving the family car, my actions up and down the street in taking pictures became conspicuous to five elderly gentlemen sitting unnoticed under the shade of a large tree. I sense that my movements had become the subject of their conversation, and after completing my chore, I approached the group, introducing myself and explaining the purpose of visiting their town of Marshall. They were all in their sixties and seventies, and possessed the charm and cordiality of real country folks. They pleaded ignorance to the exploits of William Archer, knowing only that the marker in the town square acknowledged that he did found their town in 1835. My revelations of the Colonel's activities in the Chicagoland area did stimulate their reminiscences, as one of the men pointed to the town hotel across the street, and said that he remembered that it was once called the Archer hotel, before being changed to Marshall. Another of the group related that legend had it that Abraham Lincoln used the hotel as a frequent stop-over place. I asked them if the town had an old jail house, the property of which Archer had donated to Marshall. Sheepishly, they informed me that the building still stood, and was still in use as the town's prison lock-up.

Marshall is historically located at the junction with the Lincoln National Memorial Highway that was routed by a commission, appointed to determine the much disputed path of the Lincoln family, in moving from Indiana to Illinois in 1830. From the Indiana line to Decatur, it closely follows the route of their migration, winding solely to trace a historical route. When Abe Lincoln passed through the prairie where the town of Marshall was to rise, thirty-eight year old William Archer had settled their thirteen years before, neither realizing then that in

1856, their paths would cross again, when Archer introduced Lincoln as his nominee for the vice-presidency of the United States. The Lincoln National Memorial Highway is not to be confused with the National Road, Route 40, a major transcontinental highway, also passing through Marshall. The latter followed the old Cumberland Road, constructed by the Federal government more than a century ago, at a cost of seven million dollars. At that time it was the longest continuous highway ever built in this country. The Illinois section through Marshall was built in 1837. The original Route 40, passing through the town, crossed a stone arch bridge, built by army engineers as part of the Cumberland Road, one hundred years before. Each stone in the bondless type of bridge was shaped to exact proportions by hand, and clamped together with keys to prevent slipping. When this section was realigned and resurfaced in 1931, the bridge structure was also repaired. Today, traffic races across the same span that heard the creak and rumble of prairie schooners and stage coaches many years ago.

Chapter 48: Walnut Prairie

Expressing my desire to visit the burial site of Colonel Archer in Walnut Prairie cemetery, some ten miles away, as estimated by my new Marshall friends, I bid them goodbye and headed south over the same highway that had brought us from Chicago. We found ourselves driving parallel to an embanked railroad right-of-way on our left, observing the countryside on that side. After traveling the estimated distance, the site of the cemetery was momentarily anticipated, but instead, we came to a desolate junction, posted with a Walnut Prairie sign, pointing for a left turn. Turn we did, climbing the railroad embankment to cross over its tracks. The summit gave us a view of the vast open from country before us, with no cemetery in sight. Descending the railroad incline, my eyes came upon a house obscured by the shade of a very large tree, both hugging the embankment. Last, and desperate for direction, I left the car and approached the dilapidated house, and found two old men reclining on its shady porch, a scene reminiscent of the Martin and McCoy environment. My appeal for direction to Walnut Prairie fell upon the deaf ears of one, who was sound asleep. The other man did respond to my presence, but without wasting the energy to raise his body from his horizontal position. Pointing in the direction that my car faced, he told me to follow three different dirt roads for an indefinite number of miles that would bring me to the cemetery. Thanking him for his incoherent instructions, I drove down the dusty road, raising clouds behind me. Some four miles the three roads later, we were moving under a long row of low overhanging trees, when all at once we came into a clearing and found ourselves at Walnut Prairie cemetery.

There it stood at the very edge of our road, in reverent stillness, with no barriers to enclose its boundaries. Two brick pillars supported an arched ornamental iron sign that read; "Walnut Prairie Cemetery." The structure represented the burial entrance through which the deceased were ceremoniously carried to hallowed ground, from the small church standing across the road. One of entrance pillars retained the inscription "1812"; revealing when the cemetery was first established. I closed my eyes for a moment of reflection, associating the date with historical events of that day, some one hundred and forty-three years before. Most vivid was the reality that our state of Illinois came into being in that year, only six years after the Indians laid waste to Fort Dearborn and murdered its people.

Across the road from the cemetery stood a second church, an old abandoned frame building, a short distance from its successor, a modern brick structure. The old dilapidated edifice, reflecting the nostalgic era of early Illinois settlers, was encircled with a farm type barbed wire fence, preventing anyone from entering its crumbling interior. During our brief stay, we saw no one, with only the sparse farm houses visible on the distant horizon. My family and I walked back across the dirt road and entered the cemetery, moving along its paths in search of Colonel Archer's burial site. We stopped intermittently, when called by one of our party to view the early dates inscribed on many tombstones dating back to 1818. A great number of the deceased had lived nearly a century, evidence of the country's serenity that sheltered them during their many trials and tribulations in establishing a new frontier. We came upon William Archer's monument, located near the southwest corner of the cemetery, a climactic moment in my endeavor. Interred around the Colonel were quite a number of the Archer family, but our reference for William Archer had to be shared with his father, who was laid to rest these in 1822.

The weathered inscription on his small tombstone read; "Zachariah Archer, private, Pennsylvania Regiment, Revolutionary War". Far removed from any national shrine, we paid out respects in prayer, lingering long enough to embrace the memory for a lifetime; or visiting the shared plot of deceased patriots who helped make our American heritage possible. The last chapter in the life of Colonel William Beatty Archer being completed, we strolled from the cemetery to enter our family car, and moments later our last view of Walnut Prairie was lost in the swirling dust, as we sped to our distant home in Chicago.